"No marriage is perfect, yet couples can still be happy and holy. This book shows them how. The author skillfully blends stories, examples, questions, scripture references, and a solid understanding of Catholic teachings to offer an excellent resource for couples and marriage enrichment groups."

H. Richard McCord, Executive Director
U.S. Conference of Catholic Bishops
Secretariat of Laity, Marriage, Family Life, and Youth

"Congratulations to John Bosio on his new book, *Happy Together: The Catholic Blueprint for a Loving Marriage*. Eminently readable, this book is full of practical wisdom and common sense and articulates a truly spiritual approach to marriage. Married couples will recognize themselves in its pages and find realistic ways to grow in their understanding, love, and commitment to each other. This book is a treasure."

Msgr. Charles D. McGlinn
Pastor, Curé of Ars Catholic Church
Leawood, Kansas

"Very readable, easy language, down to earth, honest, great anecdotes, and not preachy or crowded with footnotes, although the footnotes offer valuable information."

William F. Urbine, Ph.D.
President, National Association of Catholic Family Life Ministers

"John Bosio has captured the essence of married couples living a life of faith centered on Jesus Christ. His helpful advice and guidance will help couples understand the essential elements of a loving relationship. He offers the simple truth of how prayer and being involved with a community of believers can transform a troubled marriage and repair relationships. Of the numerous books dedicated to resolving potential marital difficulties, *Happy Together: The Catholic Blueprint for a Loving Marriage* offers a unique perspective by bringing Scripture, liturgical ritual, and prayer into the mainstream of married life. Couples who are serious about deepening their relationship with each other and with God will find *Happy Together* a superb resource that provides step-by-step guidance and straightforward advice."

Deacon Hans M. Toecker
Chancellor, Diocese of Nashville

To my parents, Matteo and Maddalena,
to my wife, Teri,
and our children, Angela Bosio and
Laura and Robert Allen.

Each has taught me in a
unique way how to love.

Note to the reader: I wrote *Happy Together* during the past ten years while criss-crossing the globe in my travels as a corporate manager for a Fortune 100 company. The book evolved out of reflections on my own marriage and the marriages that touched my and my wife's lives. *Happy Together* is a personal journey toward understanding what marriage means to a Christian. It is my hope and prayer that reading it will bring growth and joy to your own relationship.

Second printing 2009

TWENTY-THIRD PUBLICATIONS
A Division of Bayard
One Montauk Avenue, Suite 200
New London, CT 06320
(860) 437-3012 or (800) 321-0411
www.23rdpublications.com

ISBN 978-1-58595-685-2
Library of Congress Catalog Card Number: 2008921775
Printed in the U.S.A.

Contents

ACKNOWLEDGMENTS — iv

INTRODUCTION
"I Want It My Way!" — 1

CHAPTER 1
What Do You Believe? — 7

CHAPTER 2
Once Upon a Time... — 17

CHAPTER 3
What Keeps You Together? — 32

CHAPTER 4
What about Me? — 45

CHAPTER 5
I Welcome and I Accept You — 60

CHAPTER 6
I Am Attentive and Always Truthful — 74

CHAPTER 7
I Make Room for You in My Life — 89

CHAPTER 8
I Forgive You and Ask for Forgiveness — 104

CHAPTER 9
Comfort and Help Each Other Heal — 117

CHAPTER 10
I Am at Your Service — 129

CHAPTER 11
Where Do I Find the Courage? — 144

CONCLUSION
They Lived Happily Ever After — 158

ACKNOWLEDGMENTS

One of the themes interwoven in the pages of *Happy Together* is that we are not alone. As individuals and as married couples, our lives and love stories are connected and influence one another. This book has been inspired by many people, from the many authors who have inspired me to write, to my extended family, to our friends and colleagues, to the couples I met around the world in my travels, and to the many couples I met in counseling. In these chapters the names of couples described in counseling situations have been changed to protect their confidentiality.

I want to personally acknowledge and recognize some of the individuals and couples who influenced me by sharing their stories or reading chapters of this book at various stages and giving me feedback along the way. My appreciation goes to: Fr. Dave Perkins; Fr. Steve Wolf; Fr. Pat Kibby; Fr. George Thadathil, C.M.I.; Fr. Mario Barbero, I.M.C.; Deacon Hans and Roberta Toecker; Deacon Mickey and Carol Rose; Deacon Rob and Maria Montini; Deacon William F. Urbine; Jim and Lorraine Short; Brent and Tina Wiebe; Bill and Roberta Bolus; Ron and Valerie Fleitz; Mark and Patti Caldarulo; Dave and Barb Stockwell; Chuck and Katherine Weinstein; Kim and Greg Bullington; Rosi Stewart; Gary Carson; Tom and Barb Samoray; Susan Hoefler; Paul and Theresa Bottei; Emilio and Sandi Spinosa; Jeff and Jo Ann Summers; Miriam Moore; Dr. Phil Blansett, Ph.D.; Mark and Kimberly Newcomb; Dave and Nancy Otting; Jean Humphrey; Jack and Betty McCarthy; Pepe and Yvette Nunez; Tom and Pat Ackerman; and Pete and Jerry Braud.

Special thanks to my wife, Teri, who has been my most honest critic and valuable advisor and who patiently put up with my frequent requests to read and re-read many drafts of the same chapters.

I also want to express my appreciation to the members of the Consolata Missionaries from whom I received my formation and learned to appreciate the sacramental life of the church, especially the Eucharist.

"I Want It My Way!"

"Authentic married love is
caught up into divine love."

■ VATICAN II[1]

There is no perfect marriage. There are only imperfect men and women who marry to find happiness in each other's company. Case in point:

It was a hot and humid Kansas summer afternoon and Teri and I were about to install a screen door on the front entrance of our newly purchased home.

This was our first home-improvement project after eighteen months of marriage. We had taken great care to select just the right door, so with much confidence and enthusiasm I collected the tools I needed, tore open the cardboard box, and prepared to mount the door on the frame. (I remembered how my father used to fix things around the house when I was growing up. He seemed to know what to do instinctively.) As I pulled the door out of the cardboard box, Teri frantically rummaged through the container looking for the printed directions.

"John, wait," she said. "Let me read the directions to you before you get started."

"I don't need directions," I replied. "I know what to do. Trust me!"

Teri finally found the directions and began reading them to herself. Meanwhile I was outside working on the door. I felt proud to be taking care of the physical needs of our house, and shortly thereafter I proclaimed, "Voilà, all done! See how easy it was? No need for the directions."

"Good!" Teri said. "Great job!"

I grabbed the handle to open the door but it wouldn't open. I pulled harder. Nothing budged. "What's wrong?" asked Teri. Noticing my hesitation and puzzlement, the tone of her voice changed, and she said with indignation: "I knew it! Now you're outside and I'm inside, and the door doesn't open. This is just what we need!" I was speechless.

I was still examining the door to figure out the problem when Teri stood right across from me on the other side of the screen with the directions in hand. "Listen to me!" she said as she started reading the steps aloud. "Step one....Step two: Remove the screws from the frame that keep the door from accidentally opening during shipment."

"Oops! We missed that!" I said.

Teri promptly corrected me with a righteous tone: "Don't say 'we.' *You* missed that because you didn't want to follow the directions."

"Okay, okay," I said. "I'll take the door down and start over."

As if that wasn't enough humiliation for my oversight, I also had to endure Teri's scrutiny of my every move to ensure it complied with the written directions. I was fuming inside. "Why doesn't she go in the house and leave me alone to do it my way?" The more I repeated this thought the angrier I became. You can imagine how the rest of the day went.

This incident was painful for both of us and left us with hurt feelings. As we look back at this event after almost thirty-five years of marriage, we recognize a pattern that has repeated itself many times in our relationship. It is the tug of war we carry on when we each decide, "I want it my way!" The outcome is always the same: The relationship is hurt and both suffer no matter who wins. This tug of war is rooted in selfishness.

The fact is that all couples experience this same tug of war, especially in the early years of their marriage. Many struggle with it and often let the hurt feelings keep them from enjoying each other's company. Some get stuck in it and create a miserable life for themselves. Still others, not knowing what to do, give up on the marriage. All of the pain and unhappiness caused by selfishness is unfortunate because it's unnecessary. Each one of us can learn to control our selfish tendencies and enjoy the beautiful relationship that marriage is. *Happy Together* offers you a blueprint for marital happiness. It shows you how to overcome your self-centered tendencies by learning self-giving love.

▶ A BLUEPRINT FOR HAPPINESS

Happy Together contains a blueprint for a loving marriage that is based on the Christian belief that God made the relationship of husband and wife in his own image. John Paul II explained this belief in his *Letter to Families*: "The divine 'we' is the eternal pattern of the human 'we,' especially of that 'we' formed by the man and the woman created in the divine image...."[2] And he added: "Husbands and wives discover in Christ the point of reference for their spousal love."[3] Benedict XVI reiterated this belief in his recent encyclical on love when he wrote, "God's way of loving becomes the measure of human love."[4]

Marital happiness is achieved when couples love as God loves. In this book you will learn the attitudes and behaviors that are the essence of divine self-giving love. In practicing these in your relationship, you will experience the happiness you dreamed about on the day of your wedding.

▶ HOW TO BENEFIT FROM THIS BOOK

Happy Together is an invitation to open your heart, listen to God, and let God's grace guide you in loving your spouse. It is an invitation to make your married life a spiritual journey toward each other and toward God.

The chapters that follow have been written in the spirit expressed by Pope Paul VI: "It is married couples themselves who become apostles and guides to other married couples."[5] They contain insights, personal stories, and anecdotes that couples have shared with me about their journey to follow God's call in Christian marriage.

It is my hope that your reading will prompt you to love your spouse in a way that brings the two of you closer to God and to each other. I encourage you to read these pages together. However, this joint exercise is not necessary in order for your relationship to benefit. If you cannot read the book with your spouse, read it on your own and start practicing unilaterally and unconditionally the six steps of the blueprint outlined in these chapters.

Growth in love requires making changes. Effective change always begins with each one of us individually taking the first step. Your loving actions will not go unnoticed. Your spouse will respond in kind because goodness invites goodness,[6] and "Love grows through love."[7]

To assist you in this journey, each chapter contains recommended readings from Scripture and provides questions for personal reflection or for couple exploration. In addition, chapters five through ten provide practical suggestions for introducing grace-filled behaviors into your daily interactions.

As you apply what you learn, you will become a sacrament of God's goodness to your spouse. Together, the two of you are the visible image[8] of God's love to your children, and your home becomes a patch of God's kingdom within your community.

▶ PRAYER IS A POWERFUL TOOL

Learning to love your spouse as Christ loves is a challenge that is best accomplished with God's grace and the support of your Christian community. Therefore, I encourage you to recite often the following prayer, asking God's help for you and your spouse. Pray as well for all other married couples who need God's help. Then, when you encounter difficult moments, remember that you are not alone. As the *Catechism of the Catholic Church* reminds us: "Christ dwells with them [the spouses], gives them the strength to take up their crosses and to follow him, to rise again after they have fallen, to forgive one another, to bear one another's burdens, to 'be subject to one another out of reverence for Christ,' and to love one another with supernatural, tender, and fruitful love."[9]

Prayer is a tool that opens our hearts to God and disposes us to receive God's many graces.[10] And, when our hearts are open to God, spouses feel the presence of love in their midst and experience the happiness they seek in each other's company.

Prayer for Couples

O Lord our God,
We thank you for bringing us together as husband and wife.
We ask your Spirit to open our hearts,
     and we ask your Son to teach us to love.
To grow in communion with you and each other is what we desire.
Grant us the will to welcome and accept each other,
     the perseverance to keep our promise to always be present
     to each other,
     and the generosity to give unselfishly day after day.
Grant us the humility to ask forgiveness, the courage to forgive,
     the compassion to console, and the care to heal.
Grant us eagerness to serve without expecting to be served.
With your help our unity will grow to resemble your communion,
     and our hearts will be filled with joy.
This we ask through Jesus, your Son and our brother.
Amen.

▶ ENDNOTES

1. Abbott, Walter M., S.J. *Documents of Vatican II, Pastoral Constitution on the Church in the Modern World (Gaudium et Spes)* New York: Guild Press, 1966, #48. "Authentic married love is caught up into divine love and is governed and enriched by Christ's redemptive power and the saving activity of the church. Thus this love can lead the spouses to God with powerful effect and can aid and strengthen them in the sublime office of being a father or a mother." These words summarize the essence of this book.

2. John Paul II. *Letter to Families*. Washington, DC: United States Catholic Conference, 1994, #6.

3. Ibid., #19.

4. Benedict XVI. *Deus Caritas Est*. Washington, DC: United States Catholic Conference, 2005, #11.

5. Paul VI. *Humanae Vitae*. Washington, DC: United States Catholic Conference, 1968, #26.

6. John Paul II, *Letter to Families*, #14.

7. Benedict XVI, *Deus Caritas Est*, #18.

8. "By the joys and sacrifices of their vocation and through their faithful love, married people will become witnesses of the mystery of that love with which the Lord revealed to the world by his dying and his rising up to life again." Abbott, *Documents of Vatican II, Pastoral Constitution on the Church in the Modern World*, #52.

9. *Catechism of the Catholic Church*. Washington, DC: United States Catholic Conference, 1997, #1642.
   Also: "By the very fact that the faithful give such consent, they open up for themselves a treasure of sacramental grace from which they draw supernatural power for their fulfilling of their rights and duties faithfully." Pius XI. *Casti Connubii*. Vatican City: Vatican Publications, 1930, #40.

10. "The grace of matrimony will remain for the most part an unused talent hidden in the field unless the parties exercise these supernatural powers and cultivate and develop the seeds of grace they have received." Pius XI, *Casti Connubii*, #41.

CHAPTER 1

What Do You Believe?

"As [a man] thinketh in his
heart, so he is."

■ PROVERBS 23:7 (KJV)

Jody* made an appointment to discuss her marriage. When she arrived at my office, her first words were: "I want you to help me divorce my husband." She explained, "We fight all the time, we haven't had sex for months, we don't do anything as a couple. All he does is work. I have no feelings for him. Nothing is left. Why carry on the charade?"

I asked her, "Why do you need my help to divorce your husband?"

Jody responded, "I want to be sure I am doing the right thing."

I complimented her for wanting to make the right decision, and then asked: "What does being married mean to you?"

Her answer did not surprise me. "Even though Jim* and I were married in the Catholic Church," she said, "I don't think we knew what we were doing. To me marriage is something we enter into because we are in love. If things don't work out we move on." Then, she asked rhetorically, "Aren't we

*name has been changed

supposed to be happy?" She answered her own question: "I am not happy. It's time for me to move on."

Jody was about to make an important decision based on the pain she felt and her own misguided idea of what marriage is.

"Marriage is like a house plant," she said, pointing to a vase in my office. "When a plant loses its flowers and its leaves begin to wrinkle you give it some plant food and water. You may even change the soil. You do your best to keep it alive. After that, if it continues to deteriorate, all you can do is to throw it away."

I asked Jody to describe the status of her marriage. Using the same plant metaphor, she answered: "The blossoms are gone. The leaves are turning brown and falling. It looks very sick if not dead. I am ready to throw this plant away, but I do want it revived if possible."

"Why would you want to revive it?" I asked.

She replied, "Jim and I have invested a lot of time and effort in this relationship. Jim has good qualities I once enjoyed. It would be nice if we could be friends again. I am also concerned about what a divorce would do for our two year old, Jackie."

"Does your Christian faith help you in caring for your marriage?" I asked.

She answered, "I don't really know. I know that the Catholic Church frowns on divorce."

I pointed out that as long as she and Jim were willing to work on reviving their relationship, there was hope. I told her also that I would be glad to work with the two of them to help them care for and nurture their marriage relationship.

After my first joint meeting with Jim and Jody I wrote in their file: "This couple's strength is what they believe about marriage, but unfortunately that is also their weakness."

Jody and Jim believed that their marriage was important enough to seek help to save it rather than abandon it. They believed that they could be happy together again. They also believed that divorce is not to be taken lightly because it could hurt their young daughter. All of these were beliefs that encouraged them to work at the relationship.

On the other hand, they also believed that marriage is disposable. "If things don't work out we move on," said Jody. This was a serious weakness. The possibility of walking away came back to haunt them whenever they experienced a setback. They would think about the option of leaving instead of making the sacrifices necessary to resolve their conflicts. The lure of this option sapped their energy, keeping them from going forward.

In addition, this couple was also missing the guidance and motivation that comes from a religious belief about marriage. Although they were both Catholic, Jim and Jody did not practice their faith and thus did not understand what a Catholic marriage looks like.

▶ WHAT YOU BELIEVE SHAPES YOUR LIFE

A great deal has been written about the power of our beliefs. What you believe about your marriage and about your spouse shapes the way you treat your mate and affects how the two of you treat each other during the growing pains of your marriage. Ultimately what you believe about marriage influences whether you are happy or miserable in your relationship and whether you stay married or not.

In this chapter I want to outline some of the key beliefs about marriage that come from our Catholic tradition. Embracing these beliefs will help you find happiness in your spouse's company. These beliefs are the reasons husbands and wives stay together, work at their differences, find fulfillment in their relationship, and enjoy each other.

1. Your Marriage Is Not Your Private Affair

I once heard an acquaintance tell a friend how she and her husband decided to get married. "When we decided to get hitched, we didn't say a word to anyone," she said. "Each of us had some money in the bank, and so we bought two plane tickets to Las Vegas and flew there to get married and to have our honeymoon. When we returned home we made the announcement."

She went on, "This is our life. We want to live it our own way! If others don't like it, it is just too bad!" I think this attitude toward marriage is misguided.

As a married couple you are not just a man and a woman in love doing your own thing with no consideration for anyone else. Yours is a relationship with a purpose. Its mission is greater than the two of you. When you married, you accepted a special role in society. You agreed to be a vital link in the fabric of humanity. As an individual and as a married couple, your life and your love story are connected to others who came before you and are linked to those who will come after you. Your marital happiness is important not just to you, but to all of society. Your joy has a positive impact on everyone around you, and your relationship teaches your children what marriage is about. Judith Siegel, author of *What Children Learn from Their Parents' Marriage*, writes: "The marital relationship observed by the child acts like a blueprint upon which all future intimate relationships will be built."[1]

Personally, I am grateful to my parents and grandparents for what they taught me through their example. I have learned from them that my personal life and my marriage story are not only connected to the lives of others, but are also intimately linked to God's life and God's love story with humanity.

2. Entering Marriage Is Saying "Yes"

My parents believed that their life as a couple had meaning and purpose because it had a place in God's design. Although God's plan was a mystery to them, they saw their task in life as husband and wife to say "yes" to God and God's will. They believed that their mission in life was to let God's purpose and mysterious plan be fulfilled through their love for each other. My parents were not perfect, but because of what they believed they learned to overcome their imperfections by relying on God for help.

My parents' view of life and of marriage evokes in me the image of God as an artist who is creating an intricate mosaic, a work of art made with thousands of tiny colored stones and gems forming a splendid design. Each one of us is like a colored pebble, a precious stone in the hands of the Artist. He sees the good and the beauty in each of us, and places us in his mosaic where we can play a unique role. Our task in life is not to try to understand God's grand plan, but to accept that God is the artist, and knows best where we belong. Our task in life as a married couple is to let him guide us to become the couple he intends for us to be.

Like Adam and Eve, Abraham and Sarah, Isaac and Rebecca, Jacob and Rachel, and Mary and Joseph, you and your spouse as a couple have a role to play in God's mosaic by saying "yes" to him and placing your life at his service. John Paul II underscores this reality when he exhorts couples and families with the words: "Become what you are"[2] in God's eyes. Becoming what God intends us to be is indeed the way to our personal fulfillment. It is the source of our marital happiness.

3. Spouses Are a Gift for Each Other

We Christians believe that God intends for marriage to bring joy to the human heart. We learn this in the story of creation found in the book of Genesis. We hear that God created Adam and Eve for each other so that they could complete and perfect one another and find happiness together. When God brought Eve to Adam, the man exclaimed in joy: "This at last!" Adam was exuberant because God had given him a special gift, a person who was like himself and who could meet his deepest human needs for a companion, a helper, and a mate. Eve was a gift from God to Adam and Adam was a gift to Eve. They were made for each other: to find fulfillment in each other and happiness together.

Being a gift to each other is what God desires for you and your spouse. When you see yourselves this way, you can glimpse the promise of happiness to come.[3]

Being a gift is not easy, however. As with every couple, your life is the epic of two people wanting to find happiness together and struggling to achieve it. You want to give yourself to your spouse but you stumble. You can find yourself

> » short-tempered and impatient when you should be tolerant,
> » critical and sarcastic when you should be understanding,
> » demanding when you should be accommodating,
> » deceitful when you should be honest,
> » causing pain and discomfort when you should be comforting,
> » expecting to be served when you should be serving,
> » vengeful and holding a grudge when you should be forgiving,
> » self-absorbed when you should be attentive to your spouse's needs...

...and the list continues.

Such behaviors, whether intentional or not, create discomfort and tension in your relationship. They detract from the gift that you are. They make your married life feel like you are driving on a bumpy road and keep you from finding happiness.

4. Selfishness Is the Root of the Problem

In truth, many of the potentially damaging behaviors described above are present in all marriages to some degree. What is interesting about these behaviors is that, generally, they are not caused by irreconcilable differences, or by personality disorders, or by a lack of communication or conflict resolution skills. They all stem from selfishness. Selfishness is the root cause of all marital difficulties and breakups. Selfishness is:

> » choosing to do what "I" want when "I" want, without any regard for its impact on my spouse or on the relationship,
> » placing "me" at the center of our life as a couple instead of "us,"

» a fundamental attitude that causes me to turn my back on my
spouse and keeps the two of us from being the gift that we are.

Selfishness is a big problem in marriage. It is like the ugly weed that
sprouts in a beautiful garden. If the weed is allowed to grow unchecked it
chokes every flower in the garden. If you do not control selfishness, it will
disrupt your relationship to the point of overrunning it. Like a weed, it will
choke the affection that you and your spouse have for each other. On the
other hand, to the extent that you conquer selfishness you will experience
fulfillment and joy.

To be a gift requires choosing self-*giving* instead of self-*gratification*. Doing this is especially difficult for us because we seem to have an inbred tendency to be self-centered. Thus, too often we choose to be selfish rather
than make a sacrifice for our spouse and our marriage.

5. Christ Is Our Help and Our Model

Thankfully, God, who wants us to be happy, gave us his Son, Jesus, who
stands by us, ready to help us overcome our weakness. The *Catechism* reminds us: "Christ dwells with them [the spouses], gives them the strength
to take up their crosses and to follow him, to rise again after they have
fallen, to forgive one another, to bear one another's burdens, to 'be subject
to one another out of reverence for Christ,' and to love one another with
supernatural, tender, and fruitful love." [4]

In Christ we receive not only God's graces to help us overcome our ego-
centric tendencies, but also the model of self-giving love that God intends
for husbands and wives to show toward each other. Christ's love for the
church is the paradigm of marital love.[5]

Christ's love for the people he met is described in the gospel accounts.
He welcomed them, paid attention to their needs, forgave their sins, comforted and healed them, washed their feet in service of them, and he died
on the cross for all of us.

Christ's acts of love define for us the qualities of Christian loving. In them we find the blueprint for building the relationship of husband and wife in a Christian marriage. When spouses follow the example of Jesus in loving each other, as Christ commanded us: "Love one another as I have loved you" (Jn 15:12), they are transformed into the couple that God called them to be. They become the image of God, a sacrament of divine love to each other and to their community.

▶ THE SOURCE OF YOUR MOTIVATION

When you believe that marriage gives you a role in society, that your commitment to each other is a response to God's invitation, that you are a gift to your spouse, that your happiness comes from overcoming selfishness, and that Christ is your help and your model for loving, then you are not likely to compare your marriage to a potted plant that can be thrown away. When you embrace these beliefs your marriage takes on a special meaning. Your motivation to stay together no longer comes from how you feel today, or from what is convenient for you, or from what is fashionable among your friends. Your motivation comes from the irrevocable commitment you made to each other, to God and to society. It comes from your knowledge that others need you and count on you to be a good husband or a good wife. It is this kind of motivation that will affect your attitudes and your behaviors, and will lead you to grow in love for each other and for God in spite of the difficulties you may encounter.

▶ THE BLUEPRINT

Chapters five through ten of this book identify the actions of Christ that form the blueprint for marital love. You will learn that to find the happiness your heart desires you are to

1. Welcome and accept your spouse.

2. Be attentive and truthful to your spouse.

3. Sacrifice to make room for your spouse in your life.

4. Forgive your spouse and ask for forgiveness.

5. Comfort and help your spouse to heal.

6. Serve God and your spouse generously.

As you practice these grace-filled behaviors you will overcome, with God's help, the selfish tendencies that hurt your marriage. You will become

» patient and tolerant instead of short-tempered and demanding,

» understanding instead of critical and sarcastic,

» willing to accommodate your spouse's wishes instead of wanting your way,

» honest instead of being deceitful,

» forgiving instead of holding a grudge and seeking revenge,

» attentive to your spouse's needs, instead of being self-absorbed.

It is through such acts of love that you and your spouse imitate Christ and create a relationship that reflects the divine life. In this relationship you will feel happy and fulfilled because you love your spouse the way God designed you to love.

▶ LISTEN TO GOD'S STORY

How God loves: Isaiah 54:5–10
How we are to love: Ephesians 5:25–33
The story of Jacob and Rachel: Genesis 29

▶ REFLECT ON YOUR STORY

» Ask yourself: What do I believe about marriage? What does being married mean to me?

» Which of my beliefs help me the most in my marriage? Which are a detriment to my marriage?

» What did I learn as a child from my parents about marriage? What do I teach my children about marriage through my actions?

» List actions of yours that you or your spouse consider to be selfish. Reflect on the impact that the repetition of these behaviors can have on your marital relationship.

» How is your religious faith a source of strength to you in coping with the challenges of your relationship and in nurturing your marriage?

» What role does prayer play in your relationship? Do you pray for your spouse? Do you pray together?

» Think of the most recent time when you and your spouse enjoyed a happy moment together. What did you do that brought you joy?

▶ ENDNOTES

1. Siegel, Judith P., Ph.D. *What Children Learn from Their Parents' Marriage*. New York: Harper Collins Publishers, 2000, p. xvi.

2. John Paul II, *Familiaris Consortio*, #17.

3. "Love between man and woman, where body and soul are inseparably joined and human beings glimpse an apparently irresistible promise of happiness." Benedict XVI, *Deus Caritas Est*, #2.
   Also: "In the joys of their love and family life he [Christ] gives them here on earth a foretaste of the wedding feast of the Lamb." *Catechism of the Catholic Church*, #1642.

4. *Catechism of the Catholic Church*, #1642.
   Also: "By the very fact that the faithful give such consent, they open up for themselves a treasure of sacramental grace from which they draw supernatural power for their fulfilling of their rights and duties faithfully." Pius XI, *Casti Connubii*, #40.

5. "Christ has revealed this truth in the Gospel by his presence at Cana in Galilee, by the sacrifice of the cross and the sacraments of his church. Husbands and wives thus discover in Christ the point of reference for their spousal love." John Paul II, *Letter to Families*, #19.

CHAPTER 2

Once Upon a Time...

"Become what you are."

■ JOHN PAUL II

Most couples, regardless of how long they have been married, cherish memories of their beginnings and enjoy talking about these and other key moments in their life together. Every couple has a unique story.

In this chapter you are invited to celebrate the journey you have traveled together. As you read the anecdotes that follow, recall the memorable events of your own life as a couple: the good times and bad times, the turning points, the tears and the laughter. Remember your beginnings, your adjustments, your battles, and your joys. I also invite you to recall how God has been present in each and every moment of your story. Remember that your story is part of his story and your life is a piece of his mysterious masterpiece.

▶ YOUR BEGINNINGS

Let's start from the beginning. If I asked you to tell me your story, what would you say? Would you begin with the day you first met? Would you start with your wedding day? Or, would you go back to a time even before you ever knew each other?

Whenever I go to Thailand for business I am reminded of my wife, Teri, and the story of our marriage. While in Bangkok I visit the Church of the Holy Redeemer—a church built to resemble a Buddhist temple. During my first visit there, I sat in one of the back pews, waiting for Sunday Mass to begin. I noticed a young girl kneeling in prayer by the icon of Mary located on the left side of the main altar. Her slender figure and dark hair reminded me of a young girl, who, thirty-three years before, had knelt in prayer in front of the same image of Mary. She prayed for her family and for her friends. She also prayed for a person she did not yet know. At thirteen this young girl prayed for her future husband, whoever he might be and wherever he might be in the world. That girl was Teri. Her father was in the military, and he was stationed in Bangkok during the Vietnam War.

Did you ever pray for your future spouse before the two of you actually met? Have you ever paused to think about the sequence of events that brought the two of you together?

When I think about the twists and turns that Teri's and my personal stories took in the years before we actually met, I marvel at the mysterious ways God works to prepare us to be a gift to each other.

While Teri was in Bangkok with her family, praying for her future husband, I was in a seminary in Europe, considering a vocation to the priesthood and dreaming of being a missionary in Africa, just like my uncle. When I completed my study of philosophy, my superiors asked me to go to the United States to learn English and pursue a degree in theology. I did not ask for this assignment. In fact I had never even thought of going to America. I did not speak a word of English. I looked upon this assignment as a sign of God's will. I viewed it as an adventure that would prepare me to be a missionary.

Meanwhile, Teri's father, stationed in Thailand, was reassigned back to the USA. Her family first moved to Florida and then to Louisiana where Teri attended and completed high school. During those years she was very involved in both church and school activities. She met and dated many young men. However, she continued to pray for the man who was meant to be her future life partner.

Teri's family moved from Louisiana to Chicago where her father, now retired from the military, found a corporate job. Teri, then a high school graduate, decided to continue living at home and to work for a year before starting college.

As for me, I was attending Catholic University in Washington, DC; during two summers between semesters I worked on service projects in Kansas City. I completed my theological studies, and the time neared for my ordination to the deaconate. However, I was uncertain this was the right vocation for me. The missionary life and the adventure associated with it were appealing, but the priesthood demanded celibacy, and I felt a desire to be married. I asked my superiors to allow me to take a year off to decide what I should do. A priest that I had met while working in Kansas City recommended that I spend that year as the director of religious education in a Kansas parish. He provided the contact to make this happen. I packed my bags and moved to Kansas.

A few months later, in my role as director of religious education, while I was recruiting volunteers for the parish's program, I met a young lady who wanted to be a third-grade teacher. She said she had just moved from Chicago to Overland Park, Kansas, and had started a degree program at the local community college. Her name was Teri.

The year of deliberation went by fast, during which I prayed for guidance. At the end of the year I decided that the priesthood was not my vocation and notified my superiors in Washington. I wanted to stay in Kansas to continue to serve the church in my current role. After my decision, as the months passed, I started dating and meeting young ladies from the area. Among these was the third-grade teacher, Teri. We became good friends. After an eight-month courtship we were married, November 17, 1972.

The story of how you met your spouse is probably filled with events that mysteriously brought the two of you together. Do you remember how that happened? Was it a mere coincidence that the two of you met? Or, was God at work in your life? What do you think?

▶ REMEMBERING YOUR ADJUSTMENTS

Do you remember the joy and exhilaration you felt on your wedding day and during your honeymoon? Even today, it is always a joy for Teri and me to open our wedding album and look at the pictures from those early days. But, everyone's honeymoon comes to an end. Ordinary life starts abruptly requiring adjustments that are often unforeseen and uncomfortable. What were some of the adjustments that you had to make?

One of the first adjustments all couples must make is that of learning to live together while giving one another the companionship and the personal space each needs to be comfortable. This is a process of learning to balance the "I" and the "We."[1] It is moving from a life of independence to one of interdependence. It is learning to dance the married couple's dance.

Brent, a friend of ours, shared with me how he felt when he returned home with his new bride, after the honeymoon.

> Our honeymoon had been an adventure. We drove from state to state for two weeks without a clear plan. We would drive and then stop wherever we felt like it. It was great. However, I was not used to all that togetherness. Before the wedding, I had been a wild man. I was very independent and did whatever came to mind. By the time we got back from the honeymoon, I needed some space and time to myself. I just wanted to be alone, away from Tina, just for a short time. But, I did not know how I could do that, since I was now married to Tina, and we were supposed to be together. I found myself pondering what was possible, "Do I have to tell her everything I do or want to

do? Do we have to do everything together? Can I get away by myself without telling her? Where can I go without her? What about my friends?" These were the thoughts running through my mind.

Finally, I decided I would test the limits of my freedom. I wanted to go out, so I decided I would go to Wal-Mart, by myself, just to get out. I had no plan to buy anything. I just wanted to be alone, for a while, away from the house. So, I discreetly put on my coat, making as little noise as possible. I opened the door, and said quickly, "I am going to Wal-Mart. Bye!" Before the door closed behind me, a voice replied, "Can I come too?" I hesitated. Then, I said, "Sure! Let's go."

It took me weeks before I was comfortable saying, "I just need some time alone. I want to do this by myself. Is that okay with you?"

▶ LIFE'S A DANCE

Brent and Tina were learning their couple-dance. The first steps in their dance were about learning to let each other know their personal needs and give each other space. Does this story bring back memories of similar awkward moments you faced in your early days together?

Accommodating each other's likes and dislikes was the most challenging adjustment for Teri and me in the first year of our marriage. Differences are often what attract us, but once a couple starts the marital journey together, these differences can become bones of contention. Teri and I brought together two very diverse cultures when we married. We were an Italian from a small town in northern Italy and a French/Irish American with family roots in Louisiana. One was the son of a farmer turned factory worker to make a living, the other, the daughter of a well-respected corporate leader. I had come to this country alone with $1,000 in my pocket. Teri, on the other hand, was used to the comfort of a large and well-established family.

In the early months of our marriage we came face to face with the conflicts created by our backgrounds and family histories.

One evening Teri greeted me with great enthusiasm: "I made beans and rice for dinner." She explained that it was a favorite dish from her Southern heritage. We sat at the table and she proceeded to serve a plate full of rice and topped it with dark beans.

After we finished saying the blessing, I looked at my plate and said to Teri: "Where is the meat?"

"There is no meat," Teri replied. "This is how we make it."

"This is it?" I said a little perturbed. "What kind of dinner is this? Beans and rice? Who eats like this? Are we poor?"

Teri was very hurt. Beans and rice was one of her favorite childhood meals, and I had ridiculed it. I had not appreciated her effort and her desire to share a favorite dish with me.

A similar clash of traditions took place at Christmas. The Christmas tree was the utmost symbol of Christmas for Teri, while to me, it was insignificant and a total waste of money. For me, the real symbol of Christmas was the Nativity scene, the "Presepio" as we call it in Italy. Our first Christmas came only one month after our wedding. In early December Teri started shopping for what would be "our Christmas tree." I reluctantly went along to please her but I complained that the trees were all too expensive, and I expressed my disapproval about killing a tree just to dress it up in ornaments, keep it a few days, and then throw it away. That first year, as a compromise, we ended up buying the scrawniest tree. In spite of its physical limitations Teri turned the tree into a splendor of lights and decorations. It took me four years to finally accept that Christmas in our home would have a Christmas tree. We adjusted to our differences by each making some type of accommodation. It was a compromise. We bought an artificial Christmas tree that was reusable year after year.

In the first years of your marriage did you find it difficult to live with and to reconcile your differences about food preferences, family traditions, spending time with each other's family, shopping habits, routines, priorities, and other interests?

▶ REMEMBERING YOUR BATTLES

Earlier I said that married life is like a dance. It is rhythmic, passionate, and beautiful. This dance can often turn into a tug of war, a battle for control and power. Do you remember how you and your spouse battled over such things as "my money-your money," "my job-your job," "my parents-your parents," "my turn-your turn," "my friends-your friends," and "I want-you want"? I do not remember the first big argument that Teri and I had, but I remember very clearly one painful confrontation that took place in the first year of our marriage. Not surprisingly, it was about money.

When we got married, we transferred Teri's money into "my" checking account. We thought this was the best way to handle our finances. For us, having a common account represented our intent of sharing everything. Since our money was now in what used to be "my" checking account, we both assumed that I would be the one to keep the checkbook and pay the bills. Besides, in Teri's family, her father paid the bills.

We soon ran into a problem. As I tracked the expenses, it became painfully obvious to me that Teri and I had different priorities in our spending habits. Looking at the entries in the checkbook, I would find myself questioning Teri on most purchases she made. "Was this really necessary? Do you realize how close we are to being overdrawn? Why didn't you ask me before buying that?" This type of questioning created a lot of friction between us.

The situation actually worsened when Teri lost her job. Now she was home during the day and spent more time shopping. I soon became very concerned. I would say to myself: "Not only is she not earning any money, but she is spending more, and worse, she is buying things I don't think are necessary." These thoughts upset me and led me to make sarcastic remarks that escalated our tug of war. I started watching the checkbook entries ever more closely. Teri started making some purchases just to make the point that she did not have to account to me for every dollar she spent. Tension was building up.

This unpleasant situation finally came to a resolution when we decided to have a serious talk on this subject. One evening I said to Teri: "Sometimes I feel that you expect me to provide a comfortable life for you, just like your father did when you lived at home. You used to work; now you don't, and I do not make very much money. I don't understand why you shop at the same department stores and buy the same brands your mother buys. They are so expensive!" She replied: "I know that you are not making very much money, and I will get another job soon. And, by the way, I do not expect to live like my parents do, but you are cheap. If it were up to you we would never buy anything, or we would shop at the dollar store all the time."

Needless to say, it was a long conversation in which we shared many feelings and thoughts on this matter. Finally, we agreed that we had a problem, and decided that the best solution to our dilemma was to create a budget. The next day we went out and bought a ledger. We worked together to allocate our monthly income into categories that reflected our typical expenditures: rent, food, clothing, gas, etc. We both agreed to follow the budget faithfully, and this proved very helpful.

On my part, I volunteered that Teri should keep the checkbook and pay the bills. She was making most of the purchases for both of us. It was best if she knew how much money was in the bank. In spite of my anxiety about money, I trusted her judgment and knew that she would be prudent. As it turned out, Teri is a very capable money manager.

In retrospect, I think that battles such as this, over money, sex, in-laws, children, and hobbies, are necessary evils in every marriage.[2] They help each spouse define oneself and one's role in the relationship. They also contribute to the establishment of agreements that form the landscape of each couple's marital unity. However, when, out of selfishness, these battles are used to beat each other up, the negative consequences are significant. If differences of opinions are not resolved with mutually agreeable compromises the conflicts continue. They manifest themselves in subtle skirmishes and sabotages that appear throughout the marital relationship and do much damage to the unity of the marriage.

Experts tell us that many conflicts in marriage are inevitable, and that some are irresolvable. Lasting marriages result from a couple's ability to negotiate solutions to the conflicts that can be resolved, and to agree to tolerate and live with the differences that cannot be resolved.[3] Dr. Gottmann advises couples: "You need to understand that bottom-line difference that is causing the conflict between you—and learn how to live with it by honoring and respecting each other."[4] Unfortunately, what stands in the way of achieving compromises in an honorable way is often our ego, our selfishness: our desire to have it "my way."

What Teri and I have learned from our own relationship and from observing other couples is that these inevitable battles are most critical and most painful in the first five to ten years. In fact, the U.S. Census Bureau reports that fifty percent of those who divorce do so by the eighth year of marriage.[5] After the tenth year, most of the important issues of contention are settled, and life together takes on a different pace.

Of course, nothing is permanent. New conflicts arise as married life constantly changes, especially with the birth of children. In every marriage, as time passes, new agreements must be renegotiated and commitments remade. Hopefully, with experience and time, positive habits have been created for dealing with conflicts of taste, schedules, priorities, roles, and responsibilities.

▶ REMEMBERING THE JOYS

So far, we have spoken about adjustments and battles because these are inevitable events in each couple's transition to a life in common. It is equally important to celebrate and remember the successes and the joys that accompany blending two lives into one.

As Teri and I reflect on our story, we remember with fondness simple moments, times of passion, the comfort of our friendship, and experiences of deep peace in each other's company. I remember the joys of holding hands during a quiet walk in the park, a warm welcome home after a long trip abroad, a quiet evening watching TV sitting next to each other, memorable anniversary celebrations, special trips together, our Friday night dates, and many other events enjoyed in each other's company.

Married life also has its peak experiences that make all the pains vanish. For most couples the announcement of a pregnancy or the birth of a child are examples of peak experiences. These are moments in which spouses realize concretely, perhaps for the first time, that their lives are tied to one another in a way that can never be dissolved. They become aware that, from now on, "my life" will be more than just "you and me." It will be me and you and this person who is an extension of us in history and to whom we will give love and care. This realization strengthens the emotional bond that exists between husband and wife.

I remember my first week as a father, after we brought our firstborn, Angela, home. I often checked her to see if she was still breathing. I could not believe that Teri and I were capable of providing so totally for another human being, who was helpless and completely dependent on us. I felt very close to Teri, and I felt a sense of awe for what we had done together.

Recently, Pepe, a colleague of mine who lives in Santiago, Chile, stopped by my office for a business meeting. Before we started he pulled out a picture of his two-week-old baby, Isabella. This young father was beaming with pride as he talked about his wife, Yvette, and his newborn.

I asked him, "How do you feel about having a new baby?"

He said, "I have so many different emotions. I am happy that our Isabella is healthy and beautiful. I am thankful to God that the delivery went well. I am in awe of what Yvette and I have created. I am scared of the responsibility I have taken with this child. I dream about this little baby's future and my place in it: her first words, her first step, playing with her, taking her to school." Pepe went on and on with a litany of hopes and dreams.

Do you remember the birth of your children? Do you remember how you felt when each of them was born? Did you feel a sense of awe when you first held each of them? Did you think of God and thank him for the precious gift that each child is? What changes did this event introduce into your life as a couple? What kind of stress did the birth of your first child bring to your relationship?

▶ CELEBRATING WITH RITUALS

During the years of marriage it is easy for spouses to let their relationship shift into "automatic pilot" and feel like they are slowly drifting apart. Dr. Bill Doherty, author of *Take Back Your Marriage*,[6] says that all spouses have a tendency to become distant over time. This phenomenon happens not because there is something wrong with them but because that is the natural flow of things in married life. Spouses become comfortable with each other, take each other for granted, feel the pressures to pay attention to a thousand other things, and, without realizing it, they gradually turn away and neglect each other.

To avoid drifting to the point of becoming disconnected, Dr. Doherty recommends that spouses shift out of "automatic pilot" and take control of their life. He stresses the importance of intentionally doing things that strengthen the relationship. He recommends that couples create certain rituals for themselves that help them stay focused on each other.

Marriage rituals are activities that you choose to do together with your spouse on a regular basis. Doherty explains that rituals are done at regular intervals and are planned, and they have a special meaning for both of you. For example, a couple makes it their routine to spend time together each evening after the kids go to bed by playing cards, or watching a favorite show, or reading a book together. Some couples make it a habit to eat at least one meal together a day; others make Friday evening their "date night." Marriage rituals remind you that you and your spouse are important to each other, that your relationship is the top priority in your life. These rituals help you celebrate your story and nurture your relationship.

One particular event in every couple's life that is often celebrated with rituals is the wedding anniversary. How do you celebrate your anniversaries? Some couples are very creative with these celebrations. Our friend Barbara, who lives in Tennessee, told us:

> David and I take turns planning our anniversaries. One year, when it was my turn, I gave David the impression that I could not think of anything special for us to do. I reminded him that we had many expenses and we could not afford anything special. And, that was all true. But I wanted to surprise him. So, when the day came I took the kids to a friend's house, packed a suitcase for both of us, ordered a limousine, and had the driver take me to David's work to pick him up. Just imagine the surprise on David's face and his coworkers when they saw me standing next to the white stretch limo!
>
> After the shock wore off, I asked him to get in, and the driver pulled away without saying where we were going. David was even more shocked when we drove up to the lobby of the Opryland Hotel in Nashville, and we were escorted to the presidential suite, the most expensive room in the whole hotel. I can still hear David asking me over and over, "Can we afford this?" It truly was a great way to celebrate "us." We had a wonderful weekend together. Just the two of us.

Commemorating your anniversaries and creating rituals for yourselves are important ways to remember your story and to celebrate what the two of you mean to each other. These celebrations do not need to be fancy or expensive. They need to be occasions on which you intentionally say "thank you" to your spouse for the gift that he or she is to you. Remember, today's events are tomorrow's memories. Anniversary celebrations are also occasions for you to turn to God and to thank him for his presence in your life.

As we conclude this chapter I invite you to schedule a date with your spouse during which you revisit your story. Use the questions below as springboards for intimate conversation. To help you in this exercise, you may also want to look at photos or picture albums, starting from the early days through today.

As you travel down memory lane with your spouse, notice how your love story is an unfolding mystery. When you first met you would never have imagined all the events you have encountered together so far. The challenges you have faced together and even the battles you have fought with each other have shaped who you have become as a couple. Finding happiness is not something that happens accidentally. God calls you to "become what you are"[7] in his grand design. This requires you to make intentional choices through which you show care for your spouse and for your relationship.

In the next two chapters we will explore more specifically what it is that God calls you to become as a married couple.

Please Note

Since God's love story is the model of your love story, you will find at the end of each chapter a section called "Listen to God's Story." I invite you to look up the Bible passages cited in this section. They will give you insights into God's own passionate love for humanity, and will invite you to follow God's example in loving your spouse.

▶ LISTEN TO GOD'S STORY

Consider how Mary and Joseph followed God's call to be instruments in his story

    The Annunciation: Luke 1:26–38

    Joseph's decision to stay with Mary: Matthew 1:18–25

Consider the story of Isaac and Rebekah

    The story of Isaac and Rebekah: Genesis 24

Consider the story of Abraham and Sarah and their faith in God as a couple

    The story of the Lord's visit to Abraham and Sarah: Genesis 18:1–16

▶ REFLECT ON YOUR STORY

» Recall your story and the events that brought the two of you together. How did you meet? What attracted you to each other? Do you remember your first date? What about your first kiss?

» What do you remember about your wedding? Do you have any special memories of your honeymoon? What memories do you have of your first home, your first weeks and months together? What adjustments did you have to make?

» What have been the high points and the low points in your marriage? Can you remember times that were calm, loving, and fun? Can you remember times that were disappointing and full of pain? What major conflicts stand out in your mind? How did you resolve them?

» Do you remember the birth of your first child? How did that event affect your relationship? Do you remember the births of your other children and how they affected your relationship?

» What roles did your own parents and families play in shaping your marriage?

» What role does your faith have in shaping your marriage?

» How do you celebrate your anniversaries? Plan with your spouse how you want to celebrate your next anniversary.

▶ ENDNOTES

1. "Giving ourselves to a loving partnership while remaining true to ourselves, learning to balance 'we' and 'me,' is the central challenge of intimate relationships." Welwood, John. *Journey of the Heart.* New York: Harper Perennial, 1996, p. 34.

2. It is interesting to note that there is no single relationship style that leads spouses to a successful marriage. Each marriage is unique, and each couple has their own way of relating. Gottmann explains that couples are successful when they, in spite of their styles of dealing with conflicts, remain feeling good about their interactions. His research has shown that a couple's happiness is not found in the particular style of fighting or making up, but in having a healthy balance of positive and negative feelings and actions toward each other. This healthy balance, according to his research, is a ratio of 5 to 1. As long as there are five times as many positive feelings and interactions as there are negative, the marriage is stable and this situation is a good predictor of success. Gottmann, John, Ph.D. *Why Marriages Succeed or Fail.* New York: Simon & Schuster, 1994.

3. "If there is one lesson I have learned from my years of research it is that lasting marriage results from a couple's ability to resolve the conflicts that are inevitable in any relationship....I believe that we grow in our relationship by reconciling our differences. That is how we become more loving people and truly experience the fruits of marriage." Gottmann, *Why Marriages Succeed or Fail,* p. 28.

4. Gottmann, *Why Marriages Succeed or Fail,* p. 24.

5. *U.S. Census Bureau: Number, Timing, and Duration of Marriages and Divorces: 1996.* Washington, DC: Census Bureau Publications.

6. Doherty, William. *Take Back Your Marriage.* New York: Guilford Press, 2001.

7. "Become what you are." John Paul II, *Familiaris Consortio,* #17.

CHAPTER 3

What Keeps You Together?

"For from the beginning 'male and female he created them' (Gen 1:27). Their companionship produces the primary form of interpersonal communion."

■ VATICAN II[1]

In the previous chapter you remembered and celebrated your love story. You cherished memories of tender moments, recalled lessons learned, difficult times, and joyful events. Through this reminiscing, I hope you have reconnected with your spouse in a special way. Now you are ready to go beyond the memories and to take a look at your relationship as it is today. At the end of the last chapter we cited John Paul II's exhortation: "Become what you are."[2] Here you will explore what it is that God intends for you, and you will reflect on your progress toward becoming such.

▶ WHAT KEEPS YOU TOGETHER?

In the course of conducting marriage counseling I have often asked my clients: "Why do you stay in this relationship? What keeps you together?" Couples find it hard to answer these questions because the reasons that keep spouses together are many and complex.

Couples respond: We love each other; we have a comfortable life together; for the sake of the children; we have made a lifetime commitment; we enjoy the benefits of living together; we want someone in our life who cares; we have a need for companionship. What all these responses have in common is a fundamental truth about the marital relationship: What brings man and woman together and keeps them together is the goodness each spouse finds in the other and in the life they share. Without this experience of goodness in each other, the romantic relationship cannot start, nor can the marriage find the energy to last.

Do you remember how you felt when your spouse-to-be first caught your attention? All you saw was goodness and beauty, and this was intoxicating. Seized by that goodness you decided to spend more and more time in the company of that person. Gradually you began dreaming of a life in common that was full of promises, a "good" to be had. You married, wanting to embrace and be embraced by such goodness.

I remember the day when my heart was captured by the beauty and the goodness of the person whom I would later accept to be my wife. She and I worked in the same building and I would see her often. I had noticed her slender figure, dark long hair, and her gentle manners. She was intelligent, pretty, kind, and had a certain sex appeal that made her interesting to me.

From time to time I would give her a lift home because she did not have a car. One day, during one of these brief rides, I became aware of the "two of us." My heart was struck. From that day on the image of "us" began to develop in my mind. Being around her was a pleasant experience. It was a good feeling and I wanted more of it. Soon after, I asked her out on a date, and our relationship began.

The feelings I experienced when I noticed Teri's good qualities echoed those proclaimed in the Song of Songs:

> *How beautiful you are, my love,*
> *   how very beautiful!*
> *You have ravished my heart*
> *   with a glance of your eyes.* (Song 4:1, 9)
> *Arise, my love, my fair one,*
> *   and come away.* (Song 2:10)

▶ LIVING WITH AN IMPERFECT BEING

By now, months and years have passed since your wedding, and you have had great as well as tough times together. Fortunately, when the difficult times happened you did not give up. You persisted because you realized that you could not embrace your spouse's good qualities without also embracing the human limitations and shortcomings that are part of this imperfect being. You have learned to accept that life together has its pluses and its minuses.

You stay together because you are convinced that the pluses are greater than the minuses. The difference between you and those couples who throw in the towel and give up on their relationship is your conviction that, even in the darkest of moments, there is goodness in your spouse and in your marriage. This goodness is worth the sacrifice and accommodation needed to preserve it.

The beauty and the goodness you see in your spouse are the fingerprints left by the Artist when each of you was created in his image as male and female. That goodness and beauty are God's gift to you, a touch of his grace. They are the gift you promised to share with each other and to cherish together.

It is unfortunate that pride and selfishness sometimes cause you to hide your own goodness from each other, and then wonder if there is anything good left in your relationship. You may even be tempted to walk away. Don't! It is important that you try to work things out with your spouse. It is important that you let your emotions settle and you clear your mind so that you can see your spouse's good qualities.

▶ WORKING THINGS OUT

A few years ago, I was flying from Nashville to Chicago on a business trip. I had just settled down to read a book when the passenger sitting next to me said: "Excuse me, sir, are you a psychologist? I noticed the book you are reading: *The Good Marriage.*[3] Are there any good marriages?" Those questions started a conversation that lasted until we landed. My companion was eager to talk. She proceeded to tell me that she and her husband had been seeing a marriage counselor. They were presently separated, and she was hoping that they would soon get back together.

> I love my husband, Tom*. But, I cannot be around him when he loses his temper. At times I have been scared to disagree with him for fear that he would lose self-control and do something crazy. Fortunately, he has never hit me or pushed me in anger.
>
> A few months ago I made the mistake of paying more attention to a business deal than to my husband and my family. I know, it was my mistake, but his reaction frightened me so much that I moved out.
>
> One evening he came home expecting that I would be there, have the children settled, and dinner on the table. Instead he found an empty house, dinner had not been started and the children were at a neighbor's house. No one knew where I was. I had left no note and forgot to call him. When I finally got home, Tom went crazy. In anger, he broke dishes and punched a hole in the

*name has been changed

wall. I could not stay around because I was afraid that this time he would hurt me. I packed my bags, took the kids, and went to live with my mother. A week passed before Tom and I could talk to each other rationally. I started seeing a marriage counselor and eventually Tom joined me. We are making progress. Tom and I are good for each other in many ways, and we have a good life together. We just need to work out the few problems we have.

This couple survives in spite of their difficulties because they have chosen to overcome their hurt and pride and remember the goodness they possess together. Others do the same after betrayals, major letdowns, or in the face of addictions.

When you choose to remember the goodness that you and your spouse possess you find the strength to overcome mistakes and the courage to live with each other's imperfections.

Take a moment to become aware of the goodness that is present in your marriage. Ask yourself: What is it that I like the most about my spouse? What does my spouse like about me? What do I gain from being married? Are there times when I hide my goodness from my spouse? Why do I do so? How do I share the best of myself with my spouse?

The goodness that you experience in your marriage is a value to be cherished, protected, and nurtured. The feelings of joy that flow from it are a touch of heaven that every person longs to find. Let's explore what this means.

▶ WHAT ARE YOU LOOKING FOR IN MARRIAGE?

Several years ago, Teri and I helped lead a marriage preparation weekend. During one exercise the engaged couples were asked to imagine their life together in the years to come, and to draw on a poster their dreams for the future—the life they hoped to have in five years, ten years, and fifteen years.

Most of them sketched images of big homes, shiny cars, cute children, and successful careers. The poster that caught our attention in a special way was that of a young Vietnamese couple who could barely speak English. At the center of their artwork they had placed a large red heart, and in it, they had drawn a picture of themselves facing each other. All around the red heart and on a very small scale they depicted their hopes and dreams. They explained, "What we want most to have in five, ten, and fifteen years is the happiness we feel today, when we are together."

What all spouses are looking for in marriage is happiness. They dream of a happiness that comes from being each other's companions and best friends, each other's helpers, lovers, and mates. These are the goods qualities that all husbands and wives want to find in their marriage.

Your desire for joy in the company of your spouse is not a figment of your imagination or a pipe dream. It is the hunger that every human being feels. It is the longing for something that humanity once had and then lost. John Paul II tells us that inscribed in our human heart is a distant echo of the original innocence.[4] What you and all other couples are looking for in marriage is a taste, although imperfect, of the joy and the intimacy that our foreparents, Adam and Eve, felt with each other and with God in the Garden of Eden on the day of creation. Your desire for this intimacy is not only what you long for and want to find in marriage, it is also what God desires for you to have.[5]

▶ THE JOY OF THE GARDEN

The book of Genesis tells us that God, after having made the sun, the moon, and the stars, and after having brought to life trees, plants, and animals, decided to make someone who would watch over God's creation. God said: "Let us make humankind in our image, according to our likeness" (1:26). And so God made Adam, a person who, like God, desired companionship and was capable of loving. God placed Adam in the Garden of Eden to cultivate and care for it (2:15). But God noticed that

Adam was incomplete. He had no one equal to himself with whom he could interact and love, and be loved in return. And God observed: "It is not good that the man should be alone" (2:18). So God set out to make this situation good: "I will make him a helper as his partner" (2:18). God made all kinds of animals and brought them to Adam, but saw that none among them was a suitable partner. Then, while Adam was asleep, God took one of Adam's ribs and formed it into Eve, a person equal to Adam, and capable of loving. When Adam saw Eve his heart was filled with joy,[6] so much so that he exclaimed: "This at last is bone of my bones and flesh of my flesh" (2:23). In the other, each found the person who could fill their incompleteness. When they looked at each other all they saw was the goodness and beauty of their masculinity and femininity, and they were pleased. God was so pleased that God said to them: "Be fruitful and multiply, and fill the earth and subdue it" (1:28). Then, the sacred writer concludes the story with: "God saw everything that he had made, and indeed, it was very good" (1:31).

▶ COMPANIONS—HELPERS—LOVERS— LIFE GIVERS

The Genesis story is very simple, but it speaks to our heart. It resonates with every couple's dreams of a life of love and intimate communion. Most important, it tells us what every couple is looking for in marriage, and what God intends every couple to find in this special relationship of man and woman.

Between 1979 and 1980 John Paul II devoted his Wednesday morning general audiences to a series of twenty-two reflections on the message of the Genesis story.[7] The Pope observed that God created man and woman as two ways of being human that are different but complementary.[8] And they were made for a purpose: "To be with and for each other."[9] They were created to keep each other company (2:18), to fill one another's incompleteness,[10] to be partners in sharing God's creative power (1:28), and, most of all, they were created to be a mutual gift to one another.[11] This gift must be freely given and accepted, and such giving is the essence of the marital relationship.[12]

The core dynamic of the marital relationship is the reciprocal self-giving of the spouses. This self-giving has the power to transform the relationship of two individuals into an intimate union: an interpersonal communion.[13]

▶ TASTING THE DELIGHT OF THE GARDEN

Michael Shevack, author of *Adam and Eve: Marriage Secrets from the Garden of Eden*, writes that the Hebrew root of the word "Eden" means "pleasure" or "delight."[14] When our life together as husband and wife is an interpersonal communion we feel immense delight, a feeling of joy that gives us the energy and the courage to face together whatever lies ahead.

Think of the exuberance of young lovers. They look at their future together with great optimism. Young couples preparing for marriage often say that there is no obstacle they cannot overcome together.

Think also of the passion of a man and woman delighting in their mutual attraction in sexual intercourse. They desire so much to give themselves to each other that they open themselves up to God and place themselves at his service as co-creators of new life. Because of the delight they feel in each other's self-giving they are not afraid to accept the demanding responsibility of parenthood. Later, as the child grows, these parents will draw from their communion the energy that parenting requires. They will find the courage to make innumerable daily sacrifices for the good of their family.

The exuberance, the passion, and the courage that a couple's interpersonal communion generates is a powerful force in their life. There is truly no obstacle that spouses who are in communion cannot overcome together. Not even the dark specter of death can prevail over the delight they feel in each other's presence. Consider the following anecdote shared with me by a friend.

The hospice nurse told us that Dad was approaching the final stages and the end was very near. Mom would spend as much time as she could by his side. One evening, as I walked into their bedroom, I witnessed a scene that touched my heart and left in my mind a vivid image of their deep love for each other.

The light was dimmed but the room was filled with music. Mom was sitting next to Dad's bed. She was playing some of their favorite songs for him, and she was singing along. She was singing to him the love songs that they had sung throughout their life together: "Let Me Call You Sweetheart," "I'll Be Loving You Always," "You Were Meant for Me," and many others. Dad was singing along with her, but not with his voice. He was too weak to do so. He was singing with his eyes. His face was focused on Mom as if to join her in song and in the common memories the melodies evoked. He looked at her with a gaze that embraced her and told her of his love for her. In those moments, nothing else seemed to matter to them. They were in each other's total presence, reminiscing a life of love through the songs they had sung together. They were enjoying the pleasures of their special relationship, even in the presence of an imminent death.

Looking at them side by side in this moment of sorrow, I felt their bond growing even stronger. Mom was comforting Dad and herself with her singing. As I observed their love, tears kept streaming down my face. I didn't want them to lose each other.

When your relationship is an interpersonal communion what you feel is a taste of Eden and a touch of heaven. Jean Vanier describes interpersonal communion with the following words: "The desire in the heart of every human being is to find communion and tenderness, a feeling of loving and being loved through a physical presence. Communion is the gift of self, and through this gift comes immense joy and even a form of ecstasy."[15] I believe that this ecstasy and delight in your spouse's company is what you were looking for when you said to each other "Let's get married," and you walked to the altar and proclaimed, "I do."

▶ YOUR WEDDING, A NEW CREATION

Your wedding day was a day of new creation. On that day, in God's presence and surrounded by family and friends, you promised each other to become one, to become the communion that God created you to be. You said to your spouse: "I take you to be my spouse. I promise to be true to you in good times and in bad, in sickness and in health. I will love you and honor you all the days of my life."[16] Do you remember your vows?

With those words, you launched your journey toward each other to become one, to become for each other God's special gift as companions, helpmates, and lifegivers, and you promised to always be "with" and "for" each other.

You entered marriage to fulfill your heart's deepest longing: to be in communion. Your journey continues today. It is full of promises, but the road to communion is not easy, as you well know. You want to love your spouse but you falter. Too often you are impatient when you should be tolerant, critical when you should be understanding, demanding when you should be giving, deceitful when you should be honest, self-serving when you should be serving your spouse, vengeful when you should forgive.

On your wedding day, you promised to be "with" and "for" your spouse, but, often, spouses choose to turn away from and ignore each other. This is what gets in the way of happiness. This weakness is the weight of our inheritance as children of Adam and Eve, the price of their sin. In the next chapter we will explore this weakness and its antidote, the practice of Christian love.

In summary, what keeps you together and gives you happiness in marriage is your ability to share your own goodness as a gift to your spouse. Such self-giving is what transforms the two of you into an interpersonal communion and gives you joy. In chapters five through ten you will learn the attitudes and behaviors that lead you to grow in your communion and increase the happiness you feel in your relationship.

▶ LISTEN TO GOD'S STORY

The creation of the first couple
> The first story of creation: Genesis, Chapter 1
> The second story of creation: Genesis, Chapter 2

The goodness and permanence of love
> Love is as strong as death: Song of Songs 2:8–16 and 8:6–7

The qualities of spouses
> The good wife and a joyful husband: Sirach 26:1–4, 16–21

▶ REFLECT ON YOUR STORY

» What is the good that you saw in your spouse when you first met? List five qualities you appreciate in your spouse today. What do you like most about being married?

» How are your needs for a companion, helper, lover, and mate fulfilled in your relationship? What needs haven't yet been met? Have you discussed these with your spouse?

» How do you think that you meet your spouse's needs for a companion, helper, lover, and mate? Ask your spouse to tell you how aware you seem to be of his or her needs.

» Explain in your own words what it means for you to be "with" and "for" your spouse in the routines of your daily life.

» How do you let your selfishness keep you from achieving the closeness and unity that you desire with your spouse? List on a piece of paper your selfish behaviors: What you do or say that keeps you from being "with" and "for" your spouse.

» Write God a thank-you note for the gift he gave you in your spouse.

▶ ENDNOTES

1. Abbott, Walter M., S.J. *Documents of Vatican II, The Church Today*, #12.

2. John Paul II, *Familiaris Consortio*, #17.

3. Wallerstein, Judith S., and Sandra Blakeslee. *The Good Marriage*. New York: Warner Books, 1996.

4.. "After original sin, man and woman will lose the grace of original innocence. This discovery of the nuptial meaning of the body will cease to be for them a simple reality of revelation and grace. However, this meaning will remain as a commitment given to man by the ethos of innocence, inscribed in the depth of the human heart, as a distant echo of original innocence." John Paul II (General Audience, February 20, 1980). *Original Unity of Man and Woman: Man Enters the World as a Subject of Truth and Love.*

5. "The marriage of our first parents [is] the prototype of every future marriage." Pius XI, *Casti Connubii*, #34.
   Also: "Formed in the image of God...the first man and first woman must constitute the beginning and the model of that communion for all men and women, who, in any period, are united so intimately so as to be one flesh." John Paul II (General Audience, November 21, 1979). *Original Unity of Man and Woman: In the First Chapters of Genesis, Marriage Is One and Indissoluble.*

6. "'This at last is bone of my bone and flesh of my flesh' (Gen 2:23). In this way the man manifests for the first time joy and even exaltation....Joy in the other human being dominates the words spoken by the man in seeing the woman." John Paul II (General Audience, November 7, 1979). *Original Unity of Man and Woman: The Original Unity of Man and Woman.*

7. John Paul II (General Audiences, 1979–80). *Original Unity of Man and Woman: Catechesis on the Book of Genesis.*

8. "They are two ways of 'being a body'...which complement each other." John Paul II (General Audience, November 21, 1979). *Original Unity of Man and Woman: In the First Chapter of Genesis, Marriage Is One and Indissoluble.*

9. "When God-Yahweh said, 'It is not good that man should be alone' (Genesis 2:18), he affirmed that 'alone' does not completely realize this essence. He realized it only by existing 'with someone'—and even more deeply and completely—by existing 'for someone.'" John Paul II (General Audience, January 9, 1980). *Original Unity of Man and Woman: The Nuptial Meaning of the Body.*

10. Psychologists echo the same thoughts when they describe the skills needed by spouses in marriage. Salvador Minuchin, MD, writes that couples need complementarity and mutual accommodation. "They must develop patterns of comple-

mentarity that allow each spouse to 'give in' without feeling he has 'given up.'" Minuchin, Salvador, M.D. *Families and Family Therapy*. Cambridge, MA: Harvard University Press, 1977, p. 56

11. "In the mystery of creation, man and woman are a mutual gift." John Paul II (General Audience, February 20, 1980). *Original Unity of Man and Woman: Man Enters the World as a Subject of Truth and Love.*

    Also: "If the man and the woman cease to be a disinterested gift for each other, then they recognize that 'they are naked.' Then the shame of their nakedness, which they had not felt in the state of original innocence, will spring up in their hearts." John Paul II (General Audience, February 13, 1980). *Original Unity of Man and Woman: Original Innocence and Man's Historical State.*

12. "The communion of persons means existing in mutual 'for,' in a relationship of mutual gift. This relationship is precisely the fulfillment of 'man's' original solitude....In its origin, this fulfillment is beatifying. It is certainly implicit in man's original happiness, and constitutes the happiness which belongs to the mystery of creation effected by love." John Paul II (General Audience, January 9, 1980). *Original Unity of Man and Woman: The Nuptial Meaning of the Body.*

13. John Paul II, *Letter to Families*, #6.

    Also: "The communion of persons means existing in a mutual 'for,' in a relationship of mutual gift." John Paul II. *The Theology of the Body*. Boston: Pauline Books and Media, 1997, p. 61.

    Also: "Christian families exist to form a communion of persons in love. As such, the church and the family are each in its own way living representations in human history of the eternal loving communion of the three Persons of the Most Holy Trinity." John Paul II, edited by Joseph Durepos. *Go in Peace: A Gift of Enduring Love*. Chicago: Loyola Press, 2003, p. 149.

14. Shevack, Michael. *Adam and Eve: Marriage Secrets from the Garden of Eden*. Mahwah, NJ: Paulist Press, 2003, p. 63.

15. Vanier, Jean. *Our Journey Home*. Toronto, Canada: Novalis/Orbis, 1997, p. 50.

16. Champlin, Joseph M. *Together for Life*. Notre Dame, IN: Ave Maria Press, 1997, p. 74.

    Also: "The words of consent, then, express what is essential to the common good of the spouses." John Paul II, *Letter to Families*, #10.

CHAPTER 4

What about Me?

"If the man and the woman
cease to be a disinterested
gift for each other, then they
recognize that 'they are naked.'"

■ JOHN PAUL II[1]

I had just arrived in Warsaw, Poland, on a business trip and I was tired after a nine-hour flight from Chicago. I went to eat in the hotel restaurant to ward off jet lag. While there, I overheard a man and a woman talking at the table next to mine. What caught my attention was that they seemed to be arguing and they were speaking in Italian, my native language.

The woman, in her mid-thirties, said to the man very emphatically: "And what about me? What am I supposed to do? We have been married ten years. We have lived in our small city in Italy all of our life. I have a good job and a promising career and you want to move? What am I supposed to do? Should I drop everything to follow you, just because you have found some exciting job here in Poland?"

He was quiet for a long time and then replied: "I think this move would be good for us. It would be like starting over, just the two of us, away from the pressures of our families and friends. In this new job I will make more money. Besides, we talked about having a baby, and you could stay home to take care of the baby."

"Yes, I want to have a baby," she said. "But, when I do, I do not want to be in a strange city surrounded by people I don't know. I want to be around friends and family who can help me. Don't you understand how difficult this is for me? I love you and I want to be with you. But, I don't know how I can do what you are asking of me. I need to think about this."

As I listened to this couple struggling with their decision, vivid memories of a similar situation in Teri's and my life came to mind. A few years ago, after six months of being without a job and searching, I was offered a job in a rural Midwestern town. I felt I could not pass up the opportunity, even though it meant moving my family from a comfortable life in the city to a place far away from friends.

Before accepting the job, I brought Teri to visit the town where we would live. When we drove into the town, her first impression was positive. She said smiling: "This is a *Leave-It-to-Beaver* kind of town." The homes had white picket fences, the yards were well kept, and children were playing in the streets. It was a nice and a safe place to be.

Once the novelty wore off, however, Teri started crying. She could not see herself living there. Her mood changed. We became irritated with each other. I was thinking: "We are going to run out of money soon! If I don't take this job, who knows how long it will be before another good job opportunity will come along! Doesn't she understand that?"

We had scheduled three days there. But, after two days we had done everything we had planned to do, including looking for a house. There were only five houses for sale in our price range. Needless to say, it was a very difficult decision. Even though I liked the job that I was offered, I did not feel good about the situation because I knew that Teri was not looking forward to it. We returned home and spent a difficult week going back and forth with our thoughts, trying to make a decision that was best for both of us and for our family, and one with which we both could live.

You have probably had similar situations in your life. Married life is full of decisions and choices. Some are simple and easy, others, like these examples, are difficult and excruciatingly painful. All choices, big or small, impact the marital relationship. It is through our decisions that we become a gift to each other and express our love.

Surprisingly, the decisions that impact our relationship the most are often not the big ones but the small ones. Such decisions could be: whether to listen or to ignore, to compliment or to criticize, to forgive or to hold a grudge, to say "I'm sorry" or to walk away without saying anything, to speak truthfully or to lie. Whether you realize it or not, these are the small acts of everyday life that define your relationship and shape your marriage.

Your daily choices are moments in your life in which you take a stand vis-à-vis your spouse, to be with and for[2] your beloved or to be for yourself and against your spouse. The small choices you make every day are the decisions that either bring you close to each other or create obstacles between the two of you. They tell your spouse that you care, or that something else is more important to you.

▶ WE OFTEN MAKE THE WRONG CHOICE

We live in a world full of distractions that vie for our attention: the images on the TV draw our eyes, the radio fills the air with sounds, the phone is ringing, a child is crying, our spouse is calling, the calendar reminds us of appointments, work deadlines worry us. For the sake of our self-preservation our mind screens these calls for our attention with one primary question: "What is in it for me?" To survive we are naturally inclined to choose first what is good for us personally.

We sometimes forget that in marriage our choices are no longer just about "me" and "what is good for me," or "what I want." Our choices have to be based on "what is good for us," and what is good for our spouse, our relationship, and our family. When we forget this, we make choices that are selfish and tear us apart. These selfish acts cause the good feelings we have for each other to evaporate, and we drift apart. Consequently, we feel alone and disconnected and we wonder: "What am I doing here? Why do I put up with this?" This tendency to forget that others depend on us and our weakness to resist acting selfishly in the choices we make are the causes of our unhappiness and have the potential to destroy our relationship.

▶ OUR INHERITANCE

When Adam and Eve, acting out of selfishness, disobeyed God, "the eyes of both were opened, and they knew that they were naked" and felt shame (Gen 3:7). In choosing to follow their own wishes they not only turned their backs on God, but also on each other. At that moment they stopped being with and for each other. Instead, they started being separate, each looking out for oneself.

The Sacred Writer tells us that, on that same evening, when God came walking through the garden, Adam and Eve hid behind a tree because they were afraid. Adam blamed Eve instead of standing by her when God questioned him. He said to God: "The woman whom you gave to be with me, she gave me fruit from the tree, and I ate" (Gen 3:12). Eve tried to excuse herself by blaming the serpent: "The serpent tricked me, and I ate" (Gen 3:13). At the moment of their disobedience, they stopped being a gift to each other. Their attitude was no longer: "I care about you; I am here with you and for you, to love you and defend you." Instead it was: "I take care of myself and you take care of yourself." Their unity and their "we" were shattered. They felt shame and fear; they felt naked and vulnerable.

Today, as members of the human race, we are all prone to selfishness. Like Adam and Eve, we listen to the serpent, end up doing what we should not, blame our mate, and hide because we are afraid. We sin against each other and then feel shame and grow distant. John Paul II writes: "If the man and the woman cease to be a disinterested gift for each other, then they recognize that 'they are naked.' Then the shame of their nakedness, which they had not felt in the state of original innocence, will spring up in their hearts."[3]

Our selfishness is the root cause of all marital discord, why we suffer pains in our relationship and why we hurt each other.

▶ THERE IS HOPE

In spite of our tendency to be selfish and our weakness to resist such temptations, there is hope for all couples. In the chapters that follow you will learn that you can overcome your inherited weakness with God's help. The antidote to selfishness is the practice of true love, which is the antithesis of selfishness. True love is the act of being with and for each other—unconditionally. It is the love that we crave naturally because God made us for such loving,[4] when we were created in God's image. Self-giving love is the quality of divine life. It is the way God loves and intends for us to love.

▶ TRUE LOVE

True love is the love that God showed for his people, Israel, in the Old Testament. God was with them and for them all the time. We read in the Bible that God reached out to them, bound himself in covenants with them, was present to them even when they turned their back on him, cared for them, forgave them, and protected them. The Old Testament writers often describe such love by comparing it to the love that a husband should have for his wife. The prophet Isaiah describes God's relationship with his people as a marriage:

For your Maker is your husband,
    the Lord of hosts is his name;
For the mountains may depart
    and the hills be removed,
but my steadfast love shall not depart from you,
    and my covenant of peace shall not be removed,
    says the Lord, who has compassion on you. (Isa 54:5, 10)

Self-giving love is also the love that Jesus showed humanity. Through his Incarnation he came to be with us and for us. When he walked the streets of Galilee, Samaria, and Judea, he welcomed everyone who came to him, including the poor, the sinners, and the little children. He was attentive to their needs. He cured the blind and the lame and healed the sick. He served his disciples and taught them how to serve God and one another. He told his followers to forgive, and, as he was dying, asked the Father to forgive those who were killing him. Finally, he gave himself totally for us to the point of dying on the cross.

Even after his death and resurrection Christ continues to be with us and for us today through the power of the Holy Spirit. The relationship of Christ and the church, like the relationship of Yahweh and Israel in the Old Testament, is described in the New Testament as that of bridegroom and bride. Paul preaches: "Husbands, love your wives, just as Christ loved the church" (Eph 5:25). And, John Paul II writes: "Husbands and wives discover in Christ the point of reference for their spousal love." [5] Christ's relationship with the church gives us the blueprint for loving each other as husband and wife.

But what does this mean specifically? How are we to imitate Christ's love for the church in our relationship with each other? What attitudes and behaviors are we to exhibit in order to express our love for our spouse like Christ loves his bride? We can turn to the New Testament's descriptions of Jesus' love for his disciples and the people he met, as many Christian authors have done. In this book, however, we will draw on both the Sacred Scripture and the lived experience of the church, our Christian tradition.

In other words, we will identify Christ's loving behaviors not only from the narratives of the gospels but also from the way Christ continues to express his love for the church, his bride, today.

As Christians we believe that Christ continues to express his love for the church through the power of the Holy Spirit. This relationship is most visible and tangible in our sacred rites. Scholars tell us that religious rituals have always been the primary means through which humanity and divinity interact. For Christians the liturgical rituals celebrated in all churches are encounters of Christ and his bride. During these rituals Christ is present to her and, through words and symbols, he embraces, kisses, holds, heals, cleanses, and saves her. For Catholics these loving encounters between Christ and the church are experienced most tangibly in the seven sacraments: baptism, confirmation, Eucharist, reconciliation, anointing of the sick, holy orders, and matrimony.

▶ WHAT WE LEARN FROM THE SACRAMENTS

A reporter once asked a couple celebrating their fiftieth wedding anniversary the secret of their happiness together. They responded without hesitation that, through all of their trials and triumphs, it was their shared Catholic faith and their participation in the church's sacraments that helped them not only to stay together but to find joy and purpose in each other's company.

Catholic couples learn the qualities of Christian love when they gather around the Eucharistic table and when they participate in the church's sacraments.[6] When gathered as a community in prayer they hear Jesus' message: "Love one another as I have loved you" (Jn 15:12). As we celebrate his death and resurrection, we experience Christ present with us and for us.

In the sacraments Christ gives himself to us and we give ourselves to him. In this mutual self-giving we grow in communion with God and one another.[7] It is by our communion with him that we learn the meaning of true love. It is through the grace we receive from his Spirit that we find the strength to resist our tendency to be self-centered, and we learn to love like Christ loves.

▶ HAPPY BIRTHDAY FROM HEAVEN

It was Good Friday, and I was at home working in my yard. Our friend Bill called me unexpectedly saying: "John, I want to invite you and Teri to a surprise birthday party for Bert. Bert has done so much for me during my illness that giving her a party on her fortieth is the least I can do. Will you come? The party is in three weeks." Bill, the father of five young children had battled cancer for the past two years and had just returned home from a long stay at a research hospital where he had undergone a bone marrow transplant. Bert, his wife, had been by his side all this time, caring for him and had mobilized the community to assist the family in various ways during this moment of trial.

After I hung up the phone, I said to myself: "Bill must be feeling better! That's great." The following week I left for Europe on a business trip. When I returned Teri met me at the airport and said that Bill had been taken to Vanderbilt Hospital and that he was in critical condition. That night we went to see him. Bill was unconscious but was surrounded by his family and close friends. We talked to each other and to him as if he was awake. At one point, Carol, a friend of Bill's family, said to me with a smile: "Guess what Bill asked me to do? In a moment of consciousness when Bert was not around, he asked me to help him plan for Bert's birthday party. On her birthday, he wants me to take her to get a massage and a pedicure." We laughed at Bill's persistence and humor. The event was two weeks away and he wanted the party to go on even if he could not be there.

Bill died the following week, and the whole community gathered to celebrate Bill and give support to his family. But Bill had set in motion an elaborate plan to give Bert the surprise birthday of her life. The following week, on Bert's birthday, the community came together again, this time in

Bill's backyard to celebrate Bert's fortieth. It was like Bill was there running the event. Music was playing, someone was grilling chicken and hotdogs, neighbors brought a variety of delicious dishes, and children were running around playing games. Bill was a very outgoing person who loved being with people and having fun. Most of all Bill loved Bert and even as he was dying he was thinking of her. Bill gave all of us an example of selfless love.

▶ SIX STEPS ON THE PATH OF LOVE

Six key attitudes and behaviors that husbands and wives learn from Christ form the blueprint for a happy marriage. When husbands and wives practice these attitudes and behaviors they express true love for each other and find joy.

Step 1: Welcome your spouse as Christ welcomes the church. Just as Jesus welcomed everyone who came to him during his life on earth and just as Christ today in the sacrament of baptism welcomes us, his church, into God's kingdom,[8] husbands and wives are to welcome each other and to accept and respect each person's gift.

Step 2: Remain present and attentive to your spouse as Christ is to the church. Just as Jesus was attentive to those around him during his life on earth, husbands and wives are to be attentive to each other. Just as Christ binds us to himself through the Holy Spirit in the sacrament of confirmation, husbands and wives are to seal their hearts to each other with the promise of unending presence and faithful honesty.

Step 3: Sacrifice yourself for your spouse as Christ sacrifices himself for the church. Just as Jesus sacrificed himself on the cross for us and today he shares himself with us in the Eucharist, husbands and wives are to die to their selfish interests to make room for the other in their life.

Step 4: Forgive your spouse as Christ forgives the church. Just as Jesus forgave those who were killing him and today he forgives us in the sacrament of reconciliation, husbands and wives are to forgive each other and ask for forgiveness of one another.

Step 5: Comfort and help your spouse heal as Christ comforts and heals the church. Just as Jesus healed and comforted the sick and today Christ comforts and heals us in the sacrament of anointing of the sick, husbands and wives are to comfort and help each other heal through mutual support, understanding, and care.

Step 6: Serve your spouse as Christ serves the church. Just as Jesus came to serve and washed his disciples' feet, and today he calls us to follow his example in the sacraments of holy orders and matrimony, in marriage husbands and wives are to serve God, each other, their family, and their communities.

To love our spouse as Jesus loves the church, we must embrace these attitudes and act accordingly without expecting anything in return. Such is the path of love, and these are the steps through which Christian husbands and wives are called to love their spouse. This is the blueprint for a happy marriage.

▶ THE LANGUAGE OF LOVE

At this point it would be easy to exaggerate and over-spiritualize the love of husband and wife. Christian love, however, is not something abstract and metaphysical. On the contrary, Christian love is very concrete. Just as God's love was made concrete in the person of Jesus, the love of a husband and wife is expressed in the things we do each day and is experienced with our senses.

Jean Vanier writes that the language of love that leads to communion is spoken with our whole body.[9] Our words and our attentive silence, our touch and our facial expressions are all forms of communication through which we build bridges, take down our masks, reveal who we are, and reach out to one another.[10]

It is through our body that we let our spouse know that we care, that we understand, and that we trust. It is through the medium of our body that our souls connect with each other. Barbara DeAngelis, a psychologist and popular author, writes: "Your body may reach out to touch your lover's body, but in truth, it is your soul that, through the vehicle of your body, is reaching out to touch your lover's soul."[11] This is especially true in our most intimate exchanges of sexual intercourse, which is not a mere biological act,[12] but an act through which a man and woman give themselves to each other as a gift and in so doing, "rediscover the mystery of creation" as John Paul II has written.[13] Victor Frankl writes that the sexual act is for the lover the expression of a spiritual intention.[14] And the *Catechism of the Catholic Church* states that, "the physical intimacy of the spouses becomes a sign and pledge of spiritual communion."[15] Our body is the sacrament of our love, and when our love is modeled after Christ's love, our union becomes the sacrament of God's love.

▶ THE SIX STEPS

Let's summarize here the concrete behaviors and attitudes that bring the spark of divine love into the marital relationship. You bring happiness into your relationship to the extent that you say to your spouse with your actions:

1. I welcome you and I accept you.

2. I am attentive and truthful, always.

3. I sacrifice to make room for you in my life.

4. I forgive you and ask for your forgiveness.

5. I comfort you and help you heal.

6. I am at your service and at God's service.

These statements represent a love that alone has the power to transform the two of you into an interpersonal communion: Two persons who are with and for each other all the time. When you succeed in this, your relationship becomes your home, your refuge from the daily stresses, and the sanctuary where you can meet God. You will feel the joy that you dream of in marriage, the taste of Eden, and a foretaste of that eternal joy you will feel when you meet God face to face in the next life.

In the following chapters we will examine each of the six steps and we will consider how we can grow in love for our spouse by following Christ's example. This effort would be fruitless without grace from the Holy Spirit, who guides us and gives us the courage to open our heart to our spouse. God's grace gives us the strength to change our habits and behaviors. It is only with this help that we can overcome our selfish tendencies and transform our relationship into an interpersonal communion.

▶ LISTEN TO GOD'S STORY

Adam and Eve's act of selfishness
> The story of the fall of Adam and Eve: Genesis, Chapter 3

God's love for us
> How much God loves us: John 3:16

Love is...
> The qualities of love: 1 Corinthians, Chapter 13

How to love
> How husbands and wives are to love: Ephesians 5:21–33

The power of prayer
> Jesus encourages us to ask the Father for what we need:
> Matthew 18:19–20

▶ REFLECT ON YOUR STORY

>> Do you agree with the premise of this chapter that in every decision you make you choose to either be with and for your spouse or against your spouse?

>> Do you recognize your tendency to think about yourself first? Can you remember a time when you put yourself first and the consequences of such a decision?

>> Think of a recurring situation that is the source of friction for you and your spouse. Would the situation change if each of you decided to do what is good for the other?

>> Can you think of situations in which your spouse made a sacrifice in order to be with you and for you? How did you feel?

>> How does your Christian faith help you persevere and grow in your relationship with your spouse?

>> Do you ever ask God to help you in loving your spouse? What are some of the situations in your relationship that prompt you to turn to God in prayer?

>> Do you ever pray to God to thank him for your spouse? If yes, what do you say to God?

>> Write a short prayer asking God's help and guidance in expressing your love for your spouse.

▶ ENDNOTES

1. John Paul II (General Audience, February 13, 1980). *Original Unity of Man and Woman: Original Innocence and Man's Historical State.*

2. "When God-Yahweh said, 'It is not good that man should be alone' (Genesis 2:18), he affirmed that 'alone,' man does not completely realize his essence. He realizes it only by existing 'with someone'—and even more deeply and completely—by existing 'for someone.'" John Paul II (General Audience, January 9, 1980). *Original Unity of Man and Woman: The Nuptial Meaning of the Body.*

3. John Paul II (General Audience, February 13, 1980). *Original Unity of Man and Woman: Original Innocence and Man's Historical State*.

4. "God inscribed in the humanity of man and woman the vocation, and thus the capacity and responsibility of love and communion. Love is therefore the fundamental and innate vocation of every human being." John Paul II, *Familiaris Consortio*, #11.

5. "Christ has revealed this truth in the gospel by his presence at Cana in Galilee, by the sacrifice of the cross and the sacraments of his church. Husbands and wives thus discover in Christ the point of reference for their spousal love." John Paul II, *Letter to Families*, #19.

6. "This is the deepest significance of the great mystery, the inner meaning of the sacramental gift in the church, the most profound meaning of baptism and the Eucharist. They are fruits of the love with which the Bridegroom has loved us to the end." John Paul II, *Letter to Families*, #19.

   Also: "As the bridegroom rejoices over the bride, so shall your God rejoice over you" (Isa 62:5).

   Also: "The church is the bride of Christ: he loved her and handed himself over for her." *Catechism of the Catholic Church*, #808.

7. "Christ is always present in his church, especially in her liturgical celebrations.... By his power he is present in the sacraments, so that when a man baptizes it is really Christ himself who baptizes." Abbott, Walter M., S.J., *Documents of Vatican II, The Constitution on the Sacred Liturgy*, #7.

   Also: "This is the deepest significance of the great mystery, the inner meaning of the sacramental gift in the church, the most profound meaning of baptism and the eucharist. They are fruits of the love with which the Bridegroom has loved us to the end." John Paul II, *Letter to Families*, #19.

8. "In baptism the Holy Spirit leads us to Christ, and Christ opens the door to the Father." Ratzinger, Cardinal Joseph. *The Spirit of the Liturgy*. San Francisco: Ignatius Press, 2000, p. 178.

9. "The body is the fundamental instrument of communion. Communion demands a certain quality of listening, which is revealed through our attentiveness. With our bodies, with the way we look and listen, we can reveal to somebody their importance and uniqueness." Vanier, Jean, *Our Journey Home*, p. 39.

   Also: "Communion is communicated through the body, the eyes, the smile, the tone of voice, through a handshake or a hug." Vanier, Jean, *Our Journey Home*, p. 43.

10. The *Catechism of the Catholic Church* stresses this when it explains: "Conjugal love involves a totality, in which all the elements of the person enter—appeal of

the body and instinct, power of feeling and affectivity, aspiration of the spirit and of will" (#1643).

11. DeAngelis, Barbara, Ph.D.. *Passion*. New York: Dell Publishing, 1998, p. 42.

12. "Sexuality, by means of which man and woman give themselves to one another...is not something simply biological, but concerns the innermost being of the human person as such." *Catechism of the Catholic Church*, #2361.

13. "Uniting with each other (in the conjugal act) so closely as to become 'one flesh,' man and woman, rediscover the mystery of creation. They return in this way to that union in humanity, which allows them to recognize each other, and, like the first time, to call each other by name....Through it they discover their own humanity, both in its original unity, and in the duality of a mysterious mutual attraction." John Paul II (General Audience, November 21, 1979). *Original Unity of Man and Woman: In the First Chapters of Genesis, Marriage Is One and Indissoluble.*

14. "But for the real lover the physical, sexual relationship remains a mode of expression for the spiritual relationship which his love really is, and as a mode of expression it is love, the spiritual act, which gives it human dignity. We can therefore say: As the body is for the lover the expression of the partner's spiritual being, the sexual act is for the lover the expression of a spiritual intention." Frankl, Victor, MD. *The Doctor of the Soul*. New York: Bantam Books, 1971, pp. 112-13.

15. *Catechism of the Catholic Church*, #2360.
   Also: "It is also true the body that man and woman are predisposed to form a communion of persons in marriage. When they are united by the conjugal covenant in such a way as to become 'one flesh' (Gen 2:24), their union ought to take place 'in truth and love,' and thus express the maturity proper to persons created in the image and likeness of God." John Paul II, *Letter to Families*, #48.

CHAPTER 5

I Welcome and
I Accept You

Just as Christ welcomes his bride, the church, into God's kingdom you are to welcome your spouse into your life.

"Bathe this child in light,
give him (her) the new life of
baptism and welcome him (her)
into your holy church."

■ RITE OF BAPTISM[1]

R ecently the Catholic News Service reported from Rome that Italian brides and grooms marrying in Catholic churches would no longer say that they "take" each other as husband and wife, but will say that they "accept" each other. This change from "I take you" to "I accept you" emphasizes the fact that Christian spouses are to recognize themselves as a gift to each other. Gifts are to be accepted and not taken.

Welcoming one another's uniqueness and making room for each other are among the first adjustments that newlyweds make after the wedding. A couple's happiness depends on the degree of their success in this task, so the acts of welcoming and accepting each other never end. They must go on each day in the life of a couple seeking marital happiness.

▶ DISCONNECTING

Before we delve into the exploration of what it means for spouses to welcome and accept each other, let's remember the important step each spouse must take before saying "I accept you." At the beginning of every wedding there is a ritual that we could call the ritual of disconnecting.

The groom steps away from his friends and goes to the altar to wait for his bride. The bride walks down the aisle, often accompanied by her father who, on behalf of the family, kisses her good-bye and gives her away to the groom. Do you remember that moment in your own wedding?

This ritual of disconnecting is a sign of the major turning point in the couple's life. The bride and groom literally leave family, friends, and the single life behind in order to dedicate themselves to the special mission of living a life in common with another human being. In Genesis we read: "Therefore a man leaves his father and his mother and clings to his wife, and they become one flesh" (2:24). Psychologists write that unless spouses disengage from their respective families of origin, they cannot grow in their relationship with each other.[2]

With marriage we assume a new lifestyle and a new role in society. Disconnecting from our families and friends becomes a prerequisite for truly being able to welcome each other as husband and wife.

As a marriage counselor I have worked with many young couples who found it difficult to build their own life together because they had not fully disconnected either from their families or from the habits of their single life. Some had committed to the marital relationship without relinquishing the right to keep looking for other options. Others kept friends as confidants and advisors in making decisions that should be made as a couple. Still others could not move forward toward becoming a couple because they had not disengaged from the emotional or financial dependence on their families.

These situations are disastrous for the relationship because no real bond can be formed between husband and wife as long as others are allowed to interfere. Sometimes it is friends and family that do not want to let the young couple go, as in the following true story.

"Oh, No! It's My Mother-in-Law…"

It was early afternoon, the first Sunday after our wedding. Henry and I were in our little apartment and we had just come home from church. We were getting settled in for a quiet afternoon, just the two of us, when firm knocks at the door startled us. As I opened the door, my mother-in-law and Henry's first cousin pushed the door open and marched into our apartment. "Oh, no!" I said to myself. They announced that they were bringing us dinner. I was terribly annoyed. I had already planned our dinner. Most of all, I wished that they had left us alone since this was our first Sunday together in our apartment.

My mother-in-law and Henry's cousin took over the kitchen. They put dinner on the stove. Then, they went through each room—checking every drawer and every cupboard from the kitchen to the bathroom. While they did this, they chatted with each other in Italian, a language I did not understand. As the afternoon progressed, I got more and more agitated because of their behavior, and asked Henry to tell them to go home.

What was hurtful to me was the fact that Henry was not able to stand up to his mother and tell her to leave us alone. This became a big problem for our relationship in the weeks and months that followed. It was only through much soul searching and, over time, that Henry and I learned to disconnect from his family. We learned to create our own space, and make a life for ourselves independent of our families.

▶ DEATH AND REBIRTH

The disconnecting that marriage requires is a form of dying similar to what happens in most rites of initiation and in baptism.

In marriage, as in baptism, we are reborn to a new life. In baptism we die to sin and are welcomed by Christ into a life of communion with God.[3] In marriage we leave behind families, friends, and the freedom of the single life to give ourselves to our spouse and to welcome our beloved into our life so that together, we can create a new life of interpersonal communion.[4]

The dying that takes place in marriage is clearly symbolized in an old tradition still found in some wedding ceremonies today: the veiling of the bride. This veiling has its roots in ancient Greece, writes C. Kerenyi, in the book *The Mysteries*.[5] Among the Greeks, when the bride was given over to her betrothed, she was covered with a veil as if she were dead. Her groom then unveiled her during the marriage ritual, as a symbol of new life. This unveiling represented the rebirth of the spouses into married life.

▶ "I ACCEPT YOU…"

In your wedding ceremony, after disconnecting from your families and turning away from your friends, you turned toward each other and welcomed one another, each declaring the other a lifelong partner.

With the words of your vows, "I take you to be my lawfully wedded spouse," you opened your heart to welcome your beloved without conditions. This process of welcoming and accepting each other is truly the most fundamental step in your growth as a couple. It requires a conscious effort always to keep the lines of communication open, to respect each other's feelings, points of views, and preferences. It is an ongoing effort to seek to understand, to agree to disagree, and, to graciously tolerate the inconveniences we experience in sharing a life. Needless to say, it is a very demanding endeavor.

As outsiders to any marriage but our own, we are often baffled by what makes a marriage work, especially when we see spouses with different personalities, lifestyles, ideals, goals, and preferences. Just think of the many times, when observing the interactions of couples, you have wondered to yourself: "How can she stand living with him?" or "How can he stand being around her?" Yet, couples with great differences do stay together, and they are often happy. They are happy because, in spite of differences, they have learned to enjoy the goodness that each possesses. They have found a way to respect and live with each other's differences, and they have learned to tolerate or to overlook shortcomings and imperfections.

The fact is, that when you said, "I take you," and accepted your beloved to be your spouse, you promised to embrace not only what is good but also what is imperfect about this person, not only what you like, but also what you do not like, not only the good qualities but also the unpleasant traits. John Gottman, Ph.D., professor of psychology at the University of Washington, writes: "If you can accommodate each other's strange side and handle it with caring, affection, and respect, your marriage can thrive."[6]

Researchers have found that happiness in marriage does not come from having "normal" personalities but from being able to welcome and accept the qualities that each person brings to the relationship and to meld the personalities into a livable compromise.[7]

▶ LEARNING TO ACCEPT

Bringing together two individuals with different backgrounds and personal preferences into a peaceful coexistence is not something we accomplish naturally. On the contrary, we naturally resist differences because they intrude on our own way of being and doing. Therefore, we often find ourselves resisting changes that our spouse proposes. We might even try to convince or to trick our spouse into accommodating our likes and dislikes. This kind of behavior is destructive to a relationship.

Think of the last time you pushed, cajoled, bribed, tricked, or nagged your spouse to follow your way. Do you remember what happened? It is likely that your spouse felt manipulated. The result was probably tension, if not an argument, between the both of you. I share with you the following incident with Teri's kind permission. She still feels embarrassed when she thinks about the following situation.

The Empty Closet

Teri and I had been married less than six months and our life together was wonderful. One evening I came home from work and went to the bedroom to change. When I opened the closet door I was surprised to find an empty closet. It was bare. There was nothing left except my shoes. My jackets, my pants, my shirts—gone.

As I stood there in wonderment Teri came bouncing into the bedroom with a big smile. "Guess what?" she said. "This evening we are going shopping for you."

"Where are my clothes?" I asked with a perturbed voice.

"We are getting you new ones, this evening!" replied Teri with a smile.

Insistent, I asked again, "Where are my clothes?"

"I gave them away to the Salvation Army."

"You did what?" I screamed.

"You need new clothes, a new look, and I thought that as long as you had those old ones you wouldn't get new ones. So, I gave them away." She continued, "It is time to update your wardrobe! You need a new look."

At that moment I did not care about her good intentions and her explanations. I was deeply hurt because something that was part of me had been taken away without my knowledge. I was angry and protested: "These were my clothes. You had no right to give them away without my agreeing to it." Needless to say, that was a stormy evening.

Today, in retrospect, this event seems comical, a scene fit for a sitcom, and we chuckle about it. But, at the time, the exchanges were very serious. What happened that evening forced us to challenge and define the boundaries of our relationship. We discussed what belonged to both of us, what was mine, what was hers, and what was personal enough to be out of bounds to the other.

▶ RESPECT—UNDERSTANDING—GRACIOUSNESS

The process of mutual acceptance is one that continues every day of a couple's life together. It is important to take a few moments to remind ourselves of those behaviors and attitudes that contribute to our feelings of being welcomed and accepted.

I often ask husbands and wives what it is that makes them feel accepted by their spouse. Once a wife responded in a way I thought was very insightful. She said: "I feel accepted by my husband when he respects my ideas even if he does not agree, tries to understand what I want, and graciously puts up with my quirks."

Spouses express their welcome and acceptance through respect, understanding, and graciousness toward each other.

Respect

Showing respect is the first step in conveying acceptance. I am always impressed with how important showing respect is in Asian cultures. In Japan and Korea, for example, people bow to each other as a sign of respect when they meet. I am not suggesting that husbands and wives bow to each other. I simply encourage spouses to become aware of how their words and actions show respect (or not) for the person they love.

Mary* came early for her first counseling appointment. She came by herself because she said that her husband did not believe in counseling. She started our conversation with:

*name has been changed

I am here because I feel totally rejected by my husband. At home I do not seem to do anything right. Jim* disapproves of the way I keep the house. He tells me that I don't know how to discipline the children, and he even criticizes the way I dress. I feel more like his servant than his wife. Last night he brought home two of his buddies. I prepared a decent meal for them and the children, considering the short notice. During the dinner Jim started complaining to his friends, in front of the children, about my cooking. When I left the table upset, he told me he was just kidding and that I was overreacting. I am tired of being put down! He has no respect for me. He does not pay attention to anything I say. When I speak to him he does not look at me. He says he is listening but he continues reading the paper, flipping through a magazine, opening the mail, watching TV, or whatever else he is doing. I think our relationship is doomed.

It is obvious that Mary did not feel respected by Jim, her husband. He treated her as if she was incompetent, not worthy of his full attention, or deserving of his appreciation. He criticized her in front of his friends and her children. She felt humiliated and hurt. She did not feel emotionally safe around Jim. Mary and Jim's relationship was breaking down fast because its foundation, acceptance through respect, was eroding. Without each spouse showing respect for the other the marital relationship cannot be sustained.

Dr. John Gottman, a psychologist who spent over twenty years studying what makes marriages last, recommends that spouses use good manners and treat each other with the same courtesy and respect they would give to a guest in their home.[8] This is a very good suggestion we can all apply immediately. Jim did not treat Mary with the same respect and courtesy he showed his friends.

Understanding

Along with showing respect for your spouse, trying to understand is another way to show your spouse that you accept him or her. To show our desire to understand we need to put aside our tendency to be judgmental and listen with an open mind.

In my counseling room there was a long silent pause as Joyce* and George* dried their tears. I broke the silence by asking: "What are you thinking?"

"I am glad we had this painful conversation," said Joyce. "I have never understood how much it means for George to spend time with me, just the two of us. When George complained that I was gone too much, I thought he was criticizing me. I would become defensive and criticize him. Then, we would both be upset."

Turning toward George, she said: "Today, I finally realize that you have been angry because I have not been available to be good company to you."

George responded: "I did a very poor job of expressing to you what I wanted and what I was missing. Worst of all, I held my feelings inside and would explode and attack you. You are the most important person in my life, and I would like to spend more time with you, just like we used to. Do you remember how, when we were first married, we used to go for walks together or do things together and enjoy each other's company? That is what I want! I am glad you understand."

Through the mediation of a counselor this couple was able to suspend their tendency to be critical of each other and reached out to see the world the way the other saw it.

Behaviors that help you understand your spouse:

>> Keep an open mind. Don't jump to conclusions.

>> Give your spouse the benefit of the doubt.

>> Tell your spouse that you want to hear his or her thoughts and feelings, and then listen.

>> Listen attentively without interrupting.

Your words and your action tell your spouse that you want to enter their home, as Jesus told Zacchaeus, the tax collector: "Hurry and come down; for I must stay at your house today" (Lk 19:5).

Graciousness

Graciousness is a necessary virtue in marriage. Living under the same roof and depending on each other for many daily services creates situations in which spouses are bound to inconvenience one another.

Graciousness is best explained by again observing how Jesus dealt with a particular situation that occurred in his life. This situation has parallels in the life of every couple.

Luke tells us that one day Jesus went to a village with his disciples planning to have private time with them, away from the crowds. However, the people discovered where Jesus was and they came to the village. Rather than turning them away because this was not a convenient time for him, Jesus graciously chose to overlook his needs in order to tend to theirs. Therefore, he "welcomed them, and spoke to them about the kingdom of God, and healed those who needed to be cured" (Lk 9:10–11).

Doesn't this type of situation occur often in your life? What do you do when your spouse intrudes on your plans, or interrupts something you are doing? Think of the last time you heard your spouse say: "Honey, I need your help. Can you please come here?" How did you respond? Did you show displeasure for the interruption? Did you act annoyed? Did you scream at your spouse? Did you keep quiet but fume inside? Or were you as gracious as Jesus was? Of course, there are times when you cannot stop what you are doing to help your spouse, unless it is an emergency. In these situations you can explain graciously why you cannot heed the request at that very moment.

Graciousness is expressed when you respond to an inconvenience with a gesture that does not act as a putdown or as a rejection of your spouse.

Behaviors that convey graciousness:

» Be available to assist your spouse.

» Let your spouse know politely if you cannot accommodate his or her need.

As we talk about acceptance we must also recognize that there are destructive behaviors that cannot be accepted or tolerated. These should be challenged out of love for yourself and for your spouse.

▶ THE POWER OF PRAYER

You may think, "All of this is nice, but you don't know my spouse!" Yes, accepting our spouse is difficult to do. I learned from the many couples I worked with in marital therapy that prayer is a powerful tool in accepting others. When you find it difficult to accept certain annoying behaviors or personality traits of your spouse, recite the Serenity Prayer. It will help you find peace.

Lord, grant me the serenity
to accept the things I cannot change,
the courage to change the things I can,
and the wisdom to know the difference.

In time, and with the help of prayer, you will grow in your acceptance of each other's differences and idiosyncrasies and will gradually move to a different level in your relationship. You will realize how your spouse's unique preferences, personality traits, and habits add variety, charm, and zest to your life together. You will appreciate what your spouse brings to the relationship. You will say to each other, once again, as you did at the beginning: "I like you!" "I am glad I am with you!" "I love you!" "I accept you!"

▶ SIMPLE ACTS YOU CAN DO TODAY

1. Kiss your spouse good-bye in the morning and welcome him or her home at the end of the day.

2. If you have a tendency to interrupt your spouse while he or she is talking, make a conscious effort to let your spouse finish speaking, and then take your turn.

3. Be tolerant of your spouse's annoying habits. If you have mentioned several times that a particular behavior is annoying to you, your spouse is not likely to change now. Learn to accept your spouse's behaviors. Learn not to let that behavior irritate you. Remind yourself of your spouse's good qualities.

4. In your prayers ask God to help you appreciate your spouse's gifts and to overlook your spouse's annoying habits.

▶ LISTEN TO GOD'S STORY

Jesus welcomes the people: Luke 9:10–11
Jesus cures the leper: Matthew 8:1–4
Jesus and Zacchaeus: Luke 19:1–10
Jesus does not condemn the adulteress: John 8:1–11
Love one another as I love you: John 15:12–13

▶ REFLECT ON YOUR STORY

» Take a moment to recall the things that your spouse does and says that make you feel welcomed and accepted.

» Can you think of a recurring situation in which your spouse might feel rejection or lack of acceptance because of what you say or do?

» How do you treat your spouse? Can you say that you treat your beloved with the same courtesy and respect with which you treat your friends when they visit your home?

» How different are you from your spouse? What specific differences cause recurring conflicts between the two of you? How do you deal with these differences? Are you able to listen to each other respectfully? Are you able to agree to disagree and let the issue go?

» What is your routine when you leave home in the morning? How do you say good-bye to each other? Are your words and actions in those moments expressions of your love for each other? What can you change to make it an even better expression of your love?

» Review in slow motion, step by step, what happens when you or your spouse comes home at the end of the day. Who greets whom? Are the exchanges that take place in those moments making the person that is coming home feel welcomed? What can you and your spouse do differently to make those moments better expressions of love?

▶ ENDNOTES

1. *The Rites of the Catholic Church as Revised by the Second Vatican Ecumenical Council*, Study Edition. New York: Pueblo Publishing Co., 1983, p. 217. Through baptism Christ welcomes new members into the People of God. During the rite of baptism the celebrant welcomes the child or the catechumen with these words: "N., the community welcomes you" (p. 215). Later, during the intercessory prayers the celebrant prays: "By the mystery of your death and resurrection, bathe this child, give him/her the new life of baptism and welcome him/her into your holy church" (p. 217).

2. "At the first stage of the marital cycle, the young husband and wife should be deepening their commitment to each other, and drastically loosening their ties to their families of origin. Those who show evidence of clinging to their parents or siblings at the expense of their marriage relationship need to be encouraged by the marital therapist to separate from these earlier bonds or at least to alter them in a fashion that does not seriously intrude into their marriage." Humphrey, Dr. Frederick G. *Marital Therapy*. Englewood Cliffs, NJ: Prentice Hall, Inc., 1983, p. 106.

    Also: Sager, Clifford, M.D. *Marriage Contracts and Couple Therapy*. New York: Brunner/Mazel, Inc., 1976.

    Also: Boszormennyi-Nagy, Ivan and Geraldine Spark. *Invisible Loyalties*. Hagerstown, MD: Harper & Row Publishers, 1973.

3. In the prayers of petition of the rite of baptism the leader prays: "By the mystery of your death and resurrection, bathe this child in light, give him/her the new life of baptism and welcome him/her into your holy church." *The Rite of Baptism for One Child and for Several Children*. Collegeville, MN: Liturgical Press, 1970, p. 5.

4. "Interior innocence in the exchange of the gift consists in reciprocal 'acceptance' of the other, such as to correspond to the essence of the gift. In this way, mutual donation creates the communion of persons. It is a question of 'receiving' the other human being and 'accepting him....Precisely through its reciprocity, it creates a real communion of persons." John Paul II (General Audience, February 6, 1980). *Original Unity of Man and Woman: Man and Woman—A Gift for Each Other*.

   Also: "The communion of persons means existing in mutual 'for,' in relationship of mutual gift." John Paul II (General Audience, January 9, 1980). *Original Unity of Man and Woman: The Nuptial Meaning of the Body*.

5. Campbell, Joseph. *The Mysteries*. Princeton, NJ: Princeton University Press, 1990, pp. 40, 41, 43.

6. Gottman, John M., Ph.D. and Nan Silver. *The Seven Principles for Making Marriage Work*. New York: Crown Publishers, Inc., 1999, p. 14.

7. Gottman and Silver, *The Seven Principles for Making Marriage Work*, p. 13.

8. Gottman and Silve, *The Seven Principles for Making Marriage Work*, p. 158.

CHAPTER 6

I Am Attentive and Always Truthful

Just as Christ seals his bride, the church, to himself with the presence of the Holy Spirit, you are to seal yourself to your spouse with your presence.

"Be sealed with the Holy Spirit."

■ CONFIRMATION RITE[1]

The marital commitment is the promise always to be present to each other, and it requires faithfulness. This faithfulness is the cornerstone of your relationship. It is more than a promise of sexual fidelity. It is the commitment always to be aware of each other and honest with each other.

▶ MARIA

Michael* was a thirty-five-year-old insurance executive, tall and handsome with a head full of black hair. He and Carla* had been married for three years. They had no children. Michael was in the habit of stopping after work at a local bar for a drink with friends from the office. He would unwind there for about an hour and then drive home. This was something he had done for years, even before marriage.

Michael told me:

> I had become friends with many of the regulars who, after work, went to the bar at the same time I did. They were all young professionals. Some of them were married; most of them were single. We would play pool or just sit around, listen to music, drink beer and visit.
>
> One evening I stayed a little longer than usual and the bar was getting crowded. Our regular group had to squeeze tightly into a booth to make room for newcomers who had just entered and had no place to sit. During a third or fourth round of drinks, I felt a strange sensation up my leg. Someone was rubbing a leg against mine as if they were massaging it. I was surprised and looked around the table. Across from me was Maria. As our eyes met, she smiled and winked at me. I smiled back and then looked away and moved my leg, trying to ignore the incident. Maria was a petite brunette with a very dark complexion. She was beautiful and I was attracted to her. Her eyes had a twinkle, and when she smiled my heart jumped.
>
> Shortly after the incident, I left and nothing was ever said. In my mind I kept remembering her touch and her smile. I was flattered that a woman other than my wife would be interested in me. I also imagined myself responding to her, perhaps extending my leg toward her, or reaching out to touch her. Each time these thoughts appeared I would quickly chase them away. I would say

*name has been changed

to myself, "My relationship is with Carla; my attention needs to be for her. There is no room for Maria." But, especially on days when I felt distant from Carla, or upset with her, these thoughts about Maria would come back.

Several months later, my friends and I were sitting in the same booth at the bar. We had had several drinks and we started singing. I remember that everyone was feeling very relaxed. Maria happened to sit next to me this time. She leaned toward me, and as we were singing, she reached her hand over the table to hold my hand. She was gently caressing my fingers.

My emotions swelled up; my heart started beating fast. I felt good but also confused. My mind was rushing as I felt her touch. Then, I remembered Carla. I looked at my wedding ring. I squeezed Maria's hand. I turned to her, and as I smiled, I told her I had to leave. I never went back.

On the way home that evening, I bought a bouquet of flowers for my wife. This gesture was more for me than for her. I didn't do this because I felt guilty. I bought the flowers because I wanted to say to myself, "I am no longer single. Carla is part of me. She is the most important person in my life. I want to honor her with these flowers."

▶ OUR PROMISE

Let's return for a moment to the memories of your wedding ceremony. Do you remember the exchange of the rings? At your wedding you exchanged the rings as a sign of your commitment to each other, and you said: "Take this ring as a sign of my love and fidelity."[2]

The ring is a symbol with a special meaning. For many, this symbol has deep emotional roots that cling to the heart even after the spouse has gone. Ask any friend whose spouse has died, or who has gone through divorce. They will tell you of their struggle to dispose of the wedding ring their spouse gave them. It becomes for them a vivid reminder of that person and of their life together.

Now, look at the ring on your left hand. Do you know that the ring you are wearing is not yours? It is your spouse's ring. It is the ring your spouse gave you as a sign of his or her love and fidelity. The ring your spouse is wearing is the ring you gave to him or her as a sign of your love and fidelity. At your wedding you exchanged rings and made each other a promise. You promised to always be in each other's presence. The ring that is on your finger represents your spouse's presence to you and your promise to always remember your spouse.

▶ WE PROMISED TO BE PRESENT NO MATTER WHAT

Marriage therapists tell us that one of the principles of marital success is the commitment by the spouses to stay turned toward each other.[3] That is indeed what you vowed when you exchanged your rings. Your promise of love and fidelity is your commitment to always be present. It is your pledge not to turn your back on your spouse under any condition. It is your promise to always be attentive and not be distracted by other concerns or other persons.

Your wedding promise of love and fidelity was a vow to make your spouse the top priority in your life. Michele Weiner-Davis, a marriage and family therapist and author of *Divorce Busting*, writes: "The number one cause for the breakdown in marriages today is the same issue that causes infidelity. Couples aren't prioritizing their marriage. People spend time on their careers, their kids, community affairs, hobbies, and sports. But they take their spouses for granted. It just doesn't work that way."[4]

A letter to Dear Abby expresses this point well.[5]

> Dear Abby,
>   I didn't know I had a problem until the day my wife/lover/best friend walked out on me two weeks before our thirteenth anni-

versary. All our married life I worked a seven-day-a-week factory job on second shift, and in the mornings managed my own retail business. I thought everything at home was great. Our house and cars were paid for. We even owned a boat. It turns out that all my wife wanted was for me to hold her, love her, and be there for her. Now she lives six hundred miles away.

I learned my lesson the hard way. I closed my business, but it was too late. Abby, please warn your readers about the danger of becoming a workaholic. Material things are not worth the price of losing the one person who shares your life. I hope my story will save someone else's marriage.

—Hit with Reality in Michigan

Spouses who stay turned toward each other think about one another in everything they do; they keep in mind what the other likes and dislikes. They do little things for the pleasure of the other. They show interest in what the other is doing. They are aware of each other's needs and, of course, they are sexually faithful. Turning toward each other in these ways, writes Gottman, "is the basis of emotional connection, romance, passion, and good sex."[6] "Many people think that the secret of reconnecting with their partner is a candlelit dinner or a by-the-sea vacation. But the real secret is to turn toward each other in little ways every day."[7] Only when you are turned toward each other can you truly embrace one another and be in communion.

What a Fool!

Bill* is an acquaintance of mine who shared with me the following anecdote. Married twenty-five years, Bill and Teresa* have had their ups and downs while they struggled to raise their three children.

Bill said to me:

During the first fifteen years of my marriage I was one of those guys who is involved in every activity in the community. I belonged to the Rotary Club, I was a member of the Knights of Columbus and participated in all of the meetings, fund drives, and social activities of both organizations. I was also a member of the parish council. I was an usher at church. Whenever someone asked for volunteers, I was the first one to raise my hand. I wanted to be helpful to people in my community. It may seem to you that I am bragging. I am not. The fact is that I am ashamed to admit how blind and foolish I have been. But, at the time, I thought that I was doing what I was supposed to and wondered why others did not do the same. In reality, I was a fool. I was taking care of everyone else and ignoring my wife and my family.

It is only recently, during a Marriage Encounter weekend, that I finally realized what was happening. Teresa and I were sitting face to face in a hotel room trying to communicate. After a long painful silence, Teresa said to me, "Bill, I don't know you. I know what you do, and I can see that you like to help people, but I really don't know who you are. I don't know how you really feel about me. I don't know how much you love me because I seem to be the least important person in your life. Everyone else seems to come first."

That hit me like a ton of bricks. I had not heard those words from my wife before. She had probably said something like it to me some other time, but I had not been listening. Now, I heard her. I was tempted to argue, but I didn't. I took a deep breath and asked her to explain to me what she meant.

Teresa said, "You and I have not shared much time together, even though we live under the same roof and sleep in the same bed. I often wonder why I am married to you, and why you are married to me. You do not meet my emotional needs. I have to depend on my friends for this."

I found myself becoming defensive. Rather than say anything I would later regret, I sat quietly letting her words sink in. I had thought that my marriage relationship was okay. It is true that we did not spend very much time together and we did have some shouting matches from time to time, but we would always kiss and make up. Our relationship did not seem much different from that of my parents, and they were married until they died. So, what was the problem?

I asked Teresa to describe what she was expecting of me that she was not getting. She said, "I have been lonely for the past fifteen years. To cope with my loneliness, I spend time with my girlfriends. I go shopping with them, and we go to shows together. To keep busy, I teach Sunday school and volunteer at our children's school. I belong to the women's organization at church and I am very active there. Although I enjoy all of these things, my strongest wish is to be with you, to do things with you, to enjoy your company, but you are never there. When we make plans to go out, just you and me, we have to plan around your other social activities. Often you cancel our outings at the last minute because something else more important comes up. My dream is to feel important in your life—to come before everyone else you are trying to help." Then, she started crying.

The conversation went on for a long time that evening. It was a turning point in our relationship. I realized that I had been a fool. I was running around town helping people while ignoring the most important person in my life. This conversation was the greatest blessing I could have ever had. It was a painful revelation, but it has helped rearrange the priorities in my life.

I am still a member of many social organizations, but I balance my participation with time for Teresa and the children. I hope that others who do what I did can understand what I am telling you.

Some people find it so rewarding to get involved in the community, that volunteer work becomes an escape from dealing with the day-to-day drudgeries of family life. It is easier to be there for someone who appreciates what you do for them rather than being at home with your spouse who may be expecting something of you. After all, sometimes, spouses are in a bad mood, want to complain about the neighbors, or about work, or about you, or they may ask for help with the children. However, *a spouse's priority needs to be one's mate.*

What are the priorities in your life? Is your spouse at the top of your list? Making each other the priority and paying attention to one another's needs is an expression of our faithful presence to each other. It is what keeps us connected. Failing this, infidelity becomes a tempting alternative for those who feel lonely and hunger for attention, affection, and understanding from another human being.

Dr. Scott Haltzman, a psychiatrist who specializes in marriage counseling, reports that unfortunately, by age forty-five, two out of every five men and one out of every five women has had at least one affair. He adds, that for an overwhelming majority of spouses who cheat, the reason for their infidelity is not sexual.[8] What they are seeking is validation, warmth, understanding, and love.

Today, as more men and women work long hours together, it becomes easier to meet someone on the job who shows caring and understanding. It is then easy to strike up a relationship that becomes a distraction from the marital relationship. Shirley Glass, author of *Not "Just Friends,"* states in an article in *USA Today* that there is a new "crisis of infidelity" breeding in the workplace today. She says: "The infidelity is between people who unwittingly form a deep, passionate connection before realizing that they've crossed the line from platonic friendship into romantic love."[9]

Glass defines infidelity as any emotional or sexual intimacy that violates trust. In recent years Internet liaisons have become the latest threat to marriage. It's just so tempting. The Internet offers anonymity, convenience, and escape, says Dr. Kimberly Young, a psychologist and professor at St. Bonaventure University in New York.[10] Affairs that take place in chat rooms on the Internet are classic examples of emotional infidelity.

▶ OUR NEED FOR COMMITMENT

From the beginning of time, humankind has recognized the importance of commitments in relationships. Throughout history, elaborate rituals have been created and passed from generation to generation to celebrate promises made and to bind people to one another. The covenant ritual of the Old Testament is a spectacular example of this. The covenant was a ritual expressing God's total commitment to his chosen people, Israel. Through that ritual God promised to always be present to his people. He promised to be with them and for them forever and he expected the same from them.

Our model of faithful presence in the marital relationship is God. We learn from the Bible that even when humanity turned away from him, when the Israelites rejected him in favor of other gods, God remained steadfast in his love for us. His commitment to stand by us and to be present among us culminates in the mystery of the Incarnation. Jesus is called Emmanuel, which means "God among us." He renewed God's covenant through his death and resurrection.

Coming close to the end of his mission Jesus promised that he would continue to be present to his followers, the church, even after he was gone. He said: "I will not leave you orphaned" (Jn 14:18). "I will ask the Father, and he will give you another Advocate, to be with you forever" (John 14:16). This was fulfilled at Pentecost with the gift of the Holy Spirit to the church and today, to us personally, in the sacrament of confirmation.[11]

Today this New Covenant touches us personally in our celebration of the sacraments, especially the sacraments of initiation. Through baptism, confirmation, and Eucharist we are bound to God both as individuals and as members of his family. During the rite of confirmation the bishop makes a sign of the cross with oil on the forehead of the candidate and proclaims: "Be sealed with the gift of the Holy Spirit." This sealing creates an unbreakable relationship of presence between God and the Christian.

This covenant relationship between God and the church is the model for the relationship of husband and wife. Husband and wife are to be faithfully present to each other as Christ is present to the church through the Holy Spirit. It is for this reason that Christian marriage can never be dissolved (Mt 19:4–7). It is a covenant, an unbreakable union. The commitment that we make to each other becomes the bond that holds us together through thick and thin.

▶ HONESTY AND TRUTHFULNESS

Being faithfully present to each other implies another important quality in the relationship with our spouse: honesty and truthfulness. I once heard a young man say to another in a boastful way: "What my wife doesn't know won't upset her. I tell her only what she needs to know." Is this what you meant when you proclaimed to your spouse on your wedding day "I promise to be true to you"? Without honesty we cannot truly be present to each other because when we lie we hide behind masks.

There Is a Big Hole in My Heart

A couple was sitting in front of me during a counseling session. Marge*, holding back tears, began to speak: "Tom* and I have been married for twelve years. We have two children, ages twelve and nine. These have been good years. We have had our ups and downs, but in general they have been good, so I thought. Now, however, I have discovered something that has shattered my trust in Tom. I feel like someone shot a hole in my heart.

"A week ago, while I was cleaning and dusting our bedroom, I found a pile of papers on the dresser that needed to be put away. Most of these papers were Tom's. As I moved them to his desk, one caught my eye. It was a pay stub from Tom's work. I had seen these before but I had never paid attention to them. I looked at it and I was surprised by the size of Tom's pay on that stub. It was more than Tom had told me he makes."

Marge started crying. Then, turning to Tom she said, "How can I trust you? How do I know that you are not hiding anything else from me?"

I asked Tom to fill me in on what this was about. Tom very calmly explained that Marge was upset because she found out that when he gets his paychecks, he deposits a portion of it in his own account at the bank and the rest in the family account. "How much do you put in your account?" I asked Tom.

"About $600 a month," he answered.

Marge interrupted. "I am upset by the fact the you have been hiding this from me for twelve years. I thought we shared everything, including the money that each one of us makes from our job. I have never known about this private account of yours. You are holding back money from the children and me. That makes me very suspicious. I feel cheated. Most of all I am scared to find out that there may be other things you are not telling me. For all I know, you could be supporting someone else on the side."

Tom responded, "I am not hiding anything, and there is nothing devious about this. That's what all my friends at the plant where I work do. When they get their paycheck they keep some money and give the rest to the wife to manage. I need some money to play, to take you and the kids out once in a while without hurting the family budget. What's wrong with that?"

Marge, drying her tears, jumped in. "What's wrong is that you have kept this from me for twelve years. Why did you feel a need to hide this from me? Why did you not tell me this when we were first married, or all those times when we have discussed our family's finances? I've been crying because I am sad. I feel I have lost something precious this week. I have lost trust in you. I have lost some of the honesty and closeness I thought we had. Now there is a big gap between us."

There are many couples like Marge and Tom. Their relationship is infected by financial infidelity. Dave Ramsey, a financial advisor and noted radio host, told a CBS interviewer that when spouses lie about money, whether it's about spending it or hiding it, they commit financial infidelity.

Michelle Singletary, writing in the *Washington Post*,[12] reports that according to two surveys, financial infidelity is a common problem for many couples. The first survey, sponsored by *Redbook* Magazine and Lawyers.com, found that twenty-nine percent of adults between the ages of twenty-five to fifty-five and in a committed relationship reported being dishonest about their spending habits.

According to a second survey, 2005 Women & Investing Survey, sponsored by the Oppenheimer Funds, both men and women named cash as the item they were most likely to hide from their spouses. The Oppenheimer Fund survey also revealed what purchases spouses are most likely to hide from each other. For men, it was entertainment and electronics. For women, it was clothing and food. The same survey points to the fact that today there are many opportunities for financial infidelity. Many couples now maintain separate banking and credit card accounts. This makes hiding purchases from one's spouse easier. The *Redbook* survey observes that, because women are more likely to be the ones who manage the household accounts, it is easier for them to keep information from their partner, such as extra purchases or overdue credit card bills.

Truth and honesty—whether it be emotional, sexual, or financial—are an integral part of being "faithfully present to each other" because truth is an essential part of love. Love is not love unless it is a sincere gift of oneself.[13] When deceit or manipulation are present in a relationship what seems to be love is a mere game of make-believe.

Evelyn and Paul Moschetta, authors of *The Marriage Spirit*, write: "The more you uphold truth the more you feel completely at ease in each other's company. There is no pretense going on, no mind games being played, no secrets kept, no 'seeming' to be one way while inside thinking or feeling something else. There is no controlling, manipulation, or scheming to outsmart each other."[14]

Sincerity opens doors, tears down the walls that stand between the two of you, and makes you fully visible to the other. Then, each person can truly be present to the other. You can stand in front of your spouse without the need to hide, without fear of rejection, and without shame, just as Adam and Eve did in the Garden of Eden when God first brought them together.

What we are learning in this chapter is that to express our love for our spouse we must keep the promises we made when we exchanged our rings, the promise to always be present—and true presence requires honesty.

In the next chapter we will examine the third step on the path of love. In the first step we open our arms to welcome and receive each other; in the second, we embrace each other with our presence and honesty. In the third step we move closer to each other by making room in our life for one another. The relational dynamics created by these first three steps—accept, be present, and share yourself—create an interpersonal communion, a state of being with and for each other that produces the marital joy your heart desires.

▶ SIMPLE ACTS YOU CAN DO TODAY

1. Call your spouse during the day to stay in touch. Try to remember what is going on in your spouse's day: activities planned, people to meet. Ask about these events.

2. When you need to have your spouse's full attention, let them know. If they are not able to give you their full attention at that moment, schedule a time when both of you can have an uninterrupted conversation.

3. Make it a habit to go out on a date with your spouse regularly, like you did before you got married.

4. In your prayers ask God to help you be more attentive to the needs of your spouse.

▶ LISTEN TO GOD'S STORY

The new covenant: Jeremiah 31:31–32a, 33–34a
Jesus feeds four thousand people: Mark 8:1–10
Jesus promises to be with us: Matthew 28:20
Jesus promises the Holy Spirit: John 14:15–17, 25–26; 15:26; 16:7–10
The Story of Pentecost: Acts, Chapter 2
The Word dwelt among us: John 1:14

▶ REFLECT ON YOUR STORY

» What are the key ideas that stand out in your mind after reading this chapter? What is it that you want to remember?

» If you were to have a heart-to-heart conversation with your spouse what would you say to each other? Are you each other's priority? What would your spouse say that your priorities are?

» What are some of the forces in your life that distract you from giving time to and showing interest in your spouse?

» Be honest with yourself! If you were to rate your truthfulness with your spouse on a scale of 1 to 5 (1 = never, 5 = always), what would your rate yourself?

» What are the masks you wear? What are you trying to hide from your spouse?

» What routines or rituals currently present in your daily interactions are most helpful in keeping you and your spouse in touch with each other?

» Develop a nonverbal signal you can give each other when one of you feels ignored by the other.

▶ ENDNOTES

1. *The Rites of the Catholic Church as Revised by the Second Vatican Ecumenical Council*, Study Edition, p. 330. During the confirmation rite the bishop dips his right thumb in the chrism and then makes a sign of the cross on the forehead of the one to be confirmed saying: "N., be sealed with the Holy Spirit." In the sacrament of confirmation the Christians are bound more intimately to the church through the Spirit's presence in them. The introduction to the rite states: "They are so marked with the character or seal of the Lord that the sacrament of confirmation cannot be repeated" (p. 318).

2. Champlin, Joseph M., *Together for Life*, p. 76.

3. Gottman and Silver, *The Seven Principles for Making Marriage Work*, p. 79.

4. Barnes, Shirley. "Immunized Against Infidelity." *The Chicago Tribune,* August 8, 1999.

5. "Dear Abby." *Jefferson City News Tribune,* April 21, 2003, online edition.

6. Gottman and Silver, *The Seven Principles for Making Marriage Work*, p. 80.

7. Gottman and Silver, *The Seven Principles for Making Marriage Work*, p. 81.

8. Gunther-Rosenberg, Avis. "A Marriage Guru Looks at Unfaithful." *Providence Journal*, May 15, 2002.

9. Peterson, Karen S. "Infidelity Reaches Beyond Having Sex: Emotional Intimacy, Virtual Affairs Take Hold in Workplace." *USA Today*, January 9, 2003.

10. Saranow, Jennifer. "For Some Married People, Internet Dating Has Draw." *The Wall Street Journal Online*, February 12, 2003.

11. "I have said these things to you while I am still with you. But the Advocate, the Holy Spirit, whom the Father will send in my name, will teach you everything, and remind you of all that I have said to you" (Jn 14:25–26).

12. Singletary, Michelle. "Financial Infidelity—Couples Need to Be Open about Finances." *Washington Post*, October 23, 2005.

13. "Love causes man to find fulfillment through the sincere gift of self. To love means to give and to receive something which can be neither bought nor sold, but only given freely and mutually." John Paul II, *Letter to Families*, #11.

14. Moschetta, Paul and Evelyn. *The Marriage Spirit*. New York: A Fireside Book, 1998, p. 207.

CHAPTER 7

I Make Room for You in My Life

Just as Christ gives himself totally to his bride, the church, you are to share yourself and make sacrifices for the good of your spouse.

"Take this, all of you, and eat it; this is my body which will be given up for you."

■ EUCHARISTIC PRAYER[1]

Have you ever run a three-legged race? I remember as a child often participating with my friends in this fun game. A person ties one leg to the leg of another at the ankle, and then they try to run together as one unit. The pair that succeeds is the one that can best synchronize its movements so the two move together. To make progress walking while tied together, partners must suppress their natural instincts to run freely as individuals. Instead, they must learn to create a joint rhythm that allows them to advance as a unit without tripping each other and falling down.

Marriage is like a three-legged race. Spouses bind themselves to each other to run the race of their lives. Unfortunately, running the marriage race is even more difficult than running a three-legged race. When marriage brings together two strong-willed individuals with different ideas about where to go and what to do, there are likely to be many conflicts and spills. One person pulls forward while the other drags; one steps to the side and the other does not; one loses balance, pulls the other down, and the two fall. Both spouses get angry and each blames the other. Does this sound familiar?

Married life, like the three-legged race, is difficult, but it can be won. For couples to succeed at marriage they need to surrender their selfish tendencies and synchronize their wills for the sake of each other and their common good. Pope Pius XI wrote in his encyclical on marriage, *Casti Connubii*, that while God is the creator of the institution of marriage, it is the spouses who create their own marital relationship through their mutual surrender to each other for life.[2]

Surrendering one's instincts and will to the rhythm of the race, and to one another for the sake of the relationship, is truly the secret of success for anyone wanting to run the three-legged race that is marriage. Such surrendering is not easy because it demands giving up one's wishes in order to accommodate one's spouse. It may require compromising to achieve a common goal. It can also mean sacrificing one's dreams for the sake of the relationship.

Marital love is sacrificial love. The sacrifices may change in magnitude depending upon the circumstances. The idea of sacrificing for the sake of the marriage is especially difficult in the early years when we are adjusting to each other and making room in our life for our spouse's unique personality. Unfortunately, many couples falter in this process. The U.S. Census

Bureau reports that half of the divorces take place in the first seven or eight years of marriage.[3]

▶ "SURRENDER" IS A DIFFICULT WORD

The words "surrender" and "submission" have negative connotations in today's society. I imagine that you may feel uncomfortable when the words "surrender" and "submission" are applied to marriage because of the cultural context in which we live, but please continue reading while keeping an open mind.

In marriage there are two levels of submission and surrender. The first is the submission each spouse needs to make to the basic social roles that this relationship demands. The second level is the surrender that spouses must make to each other in order to become "one" as runners in a three-legged race.

▶ SURRENDERING TO WHAT MARRIED LIFE DEMANDS

Carl Jung, in collaboration with Joseph Henderson, explains in *Man and His Symbols*[4] that for a man and a woman to become a couple they must each submit to the most fundamental roles that this relationship demands. According to him, what marriage demands of a woman is obedience and submission to life's creative power over her. On the other hand, what marriage demands of a man is giving up some of his independence in order to take on his new roles and social responsibilities as a husband and as a father.

I am reminded of a conversation I once had with a couple, who after seven years of marriage were considering starting a family. The woman said: "I love my job, and I would love to pursue a career with my company, but I feel a conflict inside. While I would love to be successful in a large corporation and make a lot of money, I also feel a pull deep inside, a call to have children, and to stay home to be a mother for them. This is a call I cannot ignore. I know that there are women who claim that they can have a career and a family too. I am not sure I want to do both. In my case, I know that my family would end up losing."

This young lady's struggle is representative of the soul-searching done by many women today who try to balance career and family. A woman's call to be a mother is a voice of nature that, according to Henderson, requires submission. For men the challenge is similar. Men feel the call to provide food and shelter for their family, and to care for them in many ways. I have heard many guys explain to their friends: "I would love to go out with you and hang around like we used to, but I promised my family that we would do something together this evening."

The challenge for married men and women is learning to balance the activities that take them away from the home—work, hobbies, friends, and church or community involvement—with the needs that the spouse and the children have for their presence as a companion, parent, nurturer, and role model.

▶ SURRENDERING TO EACH OTHER

There is a passage in the Bible that causes mixed feelings when it is read at liturgy. It is Saint Paul's message to the Ephesians that proclaims: "Wives, be subject to your husbands" (Eph 5:22). While this passage was clearly understood and accepted in the patriarchal society of Paul's time, today it causes discomfort. Many of us have difficulty accepting this passage because it seems to promote a lack of equality between men and women. The passage seems to be one-sided.

The Catholic Church has always preached the equal dignity of every human being and equality between men and women. John Paul II summarizes the mind of the church on this regard with these words: "One must speak of an essential 'equality,' since both of them—the woman as much as the man—are created in the image and likeness of God."[5] However, equality does not mean sameness, or interchangeability.

Men and women are created equal but they have been assigned by God complementary roles of masculinity and femininity.[6] This concept of equality with differences between the sexes and their relationship to each other is one that John Paul II has attempted to clarify in his apostolic letter *Mulieris Dignitatem*. In this document the pope helps us understand Paul's phrase. He explains that we should understand Paul's true intent by referring to the preceding verse of his letter to the Ephesians. Paul writes: "Be subject to one another out of reverence for Christ" (Eph 5:21).

According to John Paul II, Christian spouses are equal in Christ (Gal 3:28) and are called by God to give themselves to each other in mutual surrender, just as Christ gave himself to his bride, the church.[7] Christ surrendered his life for our sake even to the point of dying on the cross. He sacrificed himself for us. "Therefore be imitators of God, as beloved children, and live in love, as Christ loved us and gave himself up for us" (Eph 5:1–2).

▶ WE EXIST "FOR" EACH OTHER

Marriage cannot exist without each spouse surrendering their time and attention to the other. Self-giving is the central attitude in a marriage. It is the attitude through which spouses empty themselves of their own ego, their own ways of doing things, their personal preferences, etc., to make room for the other person in their life. Without self-giving there cannot be fulfillment and happiness in marriage. John Paul II said it well when he wrote: "Love causes man to find fulfillment through the sincere gift of self."[8]

The practice of self-giving requires sacrifices made for the sake of the spouse. These are sacrifices that often go unnoticed because true love is not boastful, nor does it expect to be noticed (1 Cor 13:4).

Supporting my wife during her two years of school was something I wanted to do because I knew that finishing her degree was important to her. Such support of each other as a family is an expression of love. It is a giving that binds us. However, just because we want to support each other, it doesn't mean it's easy. For me, it was especially difficult when Teri's schedule conflicted with mine. There were times when I changed my plans to accommodate her need to study, finish a project, or prepare for a test. There were weekends when it would have been nice to go out, but papers were due, so we stayed home. The children also needed attention.

In every marriage there are many occasions in which spouses want to be "for" each other because they care but they feel pulled in different directions by children, work, friends, hobbies, and community and church activities. When faced with conflicting pulls and tugs it becomes easy to get sidetracked and to make selfish choices that divert our attention from what is good for the relationship. As I have said from the beginning of this book, selfishness leads us to do "what I want" without any regard for its impact on our spouse. When we follow the path of selfishness the marriage suffers.

▶ CHRIST IS OUR EXAMPLE

In his encyclical on love,[9] Pope Benedict XVI demonstrates how the Old Testament prophets described God's passion and yearning for his people, Israel, using the metaphor of betrothal and marriage. That same image becomes even clearer in the New Testament when Jesus compares himself to the bridegroom (Mt 9:15; Mk 2:19–20; Lk 5:34–35; Jn 3:29). The book of Revelation and St. Paul clearly identify Christ as the bridegroom and the church as his bride. Paul in particular makes Christ's love for his bride the model of married love when he exhorts husbands to love their wives as Christ loved the church. Christ himself commanded us: "Love one another. Just as I have loved you, you also should love one another" (Jn 13:34). Then, Christ gave up his life for us by dying on the cross.

Today, his sacrifice is reenacted in the Mass using Christ's own words: "Take and eat this is my body....This is my blood given up for you." When you follow Christ's example and sacrifice your wants, your time, your preferences to accommodate your spouse, you join Christ in his sacrifice for us. When you sacrifice for the sake of your spouse and your marriage you make room for love to grow in your relationship, and through your love you manifest God's kingdom.

A few months ago I received an unsolicited e-mail message entitled "The Meaning of Love." The author had collected many definitions of love given by young children, ages four to eight years old. Here are three that caught my attention as perfect examples of self-giving love.

> When my grandmother got arthritis, she couldn't bend over and paint her toenails anymore. So my grandfather does it for her all the time, even when his hands got arthritis too. That's love.

> Love is when my mommy makes coffee for my daddy and she takes a sip before giving it to him, to make sure the taste is okay.

> Love is when Mommy gives Daddy the best piece of chicken.

▶ GIVING WITHOUT STRINGS ATTACHED

A friend of mine told me once that he was upset because he had given his wife an expensive birthday gift and she had not shown the gratitude he expected. It is true that expressing appreciation for the gifts we receive is important, but, it is even more important to give without expecting something in return. Giving without expecting anything in return is true surrender.

There are couples who give each other gifts or do favors for each other, keeping a mental score. It is as if they go through life together keeping track of what each does: "I did this and that for you. Now you owe me!" This type of giving with self-interest kills love and brings unhappiness. It contains the shadow of selfishness. John Gottman, researcher and co-author of *The Seven Principles for Making Marriage Work*, writes: "Happy spouses do not keep a tab on whether their mate is washing the dishes as a payback because they cooked dinner."[10]

True self-giving and mutual surrender of spouses in marriage is unconditional as God's love for us is unconditional. Unconditional love is the purest form of giving. We read in the *Bhagavad Gita*, one of the sacred writings of the Hindu religion: "A gift is pure when it is given from the heart and when we expect nothing in return."[11]

▶ WHAT MUTUAL SURRENDER IS NOT

Self-giving and mutual surrender are the gift of our self for the benefit of the spouse and for the sake of the relationship. Such giving does not mean doing everything your spouse wants you to do. Self-giving does *not* mean accommodating destructive habits, doing things that go against your principles, or condoning behaviors that are demeaning to you and to your spouse. John Welwood writes, "Unconditional love does not mean having to like something we in fact dislike or saying yes when we need to say no."[12]

Mutual surrender is giving while you remain true to yourself. It is giving while you preserve your integrity. Doing this sometimes means expressing feelings and opinions that differ from your spouse's. It may mean disagreeing and exposing a problem. It may mean confronting unacceptable behaviors. Sometimes, challenging your spouse can be an act of love done for the sake of the relationship and for the sake of your spouse.

Several years ago, I met a young couple who was struggling with their lovemaking patterns. Sitting in my office during a marriage counseling session, the wife said to her husband, "Why is it that every evening you want to watch an x-rated video? You watch the video to become aroused, then you approach me for sex, and the whole thing is over in two minutes."

He replied defensively, "I have asked you many times to join me in watching the video. But you don't want to do so. If you did, you would feel differently."

She became even angrier. "You do not understand me at all. This way of making love makes me feel cheap. What about me? What am I to you? I feel like one of the actors in the video who has stepped out of the screen to satisfy your needs. I do not want to be that. I am your wife. I want to know that you make love to me because you love me, and because you want to express your love for me, not because you want to use me just to satisfy your needs. Do you understand what I feel?"

Mutual surrender does not mean that you become a doormat. If you are not a doormat and you stand up for yourself, you will experience conflicts in your relationship. The presence of conflict in your relationship is not a sign that you have problems or that you do not love each other. Conflicts are transformational moments in every relationship. They are opportunities for you to grow either closer to each other or further apart. Conflicts present you with the opportunity to truly express your love, not by giving in, but by acknowledging that you're experiencing the clash of ideas, wishes, or priorities. Conflicts give you an opportunity to seek, together, a resolution in a way that demonstrates your mutual respect and interest in each other's needs and wishes.

▶ DEALING WITH MARITAL CONFLICTS

Researchers tell us that conflicts in marriage are inevitable and that sixty-nine percent of all marital conflicts are not resolvable.[13] The problems in a marriage are not the conflicts themselves but the spouses' inability to acknowledge their conflicts and to humble themselves in front of each other by saying: "We have a problem. Let's talk about it so we can solve it. Help me understand what you want, what you think, what you feel, and what you do."

When you ask your spouse to tell you what is on his or her mind, and you listen attentively to your spouse's self-disclosure, you are truly surrendering to your spouse. For a brief moment in the three-legged race you suspend the pulling in your direction to see and hear where your spouse wants to go. You surrender your power and control. Similarly, when your spouse shares honestly with you what they think, feel, and want, they surrender to you. In so doing, they make themselves vulnerable to you. In this sharing your spouse bares his or her soul to let you see and understand what is behind his or her wishes, actions, or words.

Mutual surrender takes place when you have the courage to call timeout in the middle of a heated discussion so that you can calm yourselves down and prevent escalation. Mutual surrender is listening, it is sharing, it is exploring alternatives, and it is compromising to arrive at a solution that is acceptable to both. When you do this, you move forward on your three-legged race without faltering.

Surrendering in times of conflict is especially difficult for men, but it is crucial for the survival of the relationship. Researchers have found that husbands who are willing to listen to the suggestions and advice of their wives have happier marriages and are less likely to divorce. They write: "Statistically speaking, when a man is not willing to share power with his partner, there is an eighty-one percent chance that his marriage will self-destruct."[14]

▶ SATISFACTION IN SEXUAL INTIMACY

Mutual surrender is an essential dimension of marital intercourse. The story of the young couple with lovemaking differences describes the sad situation of a person who feels used in sexual intercourse. The wife said to her husband: "I want to know that you make love to me because you love me, and because you want to express your love for me, not because you want to use me just to satisfy your needs." Using one's spouse purely for sexual gratification is not what marital intercourse is about.[15]

When we use another person as an object of sexual satisfaction we take something from that person. Our exploitative actions are no longer lovemaking, they are pleasure seeking. Marital intercourse is not just a physical act aimed at deriving sexual pleasure from each other. It is the most intimate gift of one person to the other—a giving as a man and as a woman that fulfills each other's human nature. It is a mutual surrender that produces joy. Joy is an emotion that is greater than physical pleasure. It is the feeling that is best associated with personal fulfillment. This should not leave the impression that sexual intercourse should not be a physically enjoyable event. The *Catechism of the Catholic Church* itself reminds spouses that the physical pleasure of sexual intercourse is what God intended for them and therefore, they should enjoy it.[16]

Every act of sexual intercourse between husband and wife that is true self-giving in mutual surrender[17] is a sacramental moment. John Paul II writes that sexual intercourse manifests the goodness of God and is a celebration of God's creation of man and woman.[18]

Today's scientific research on the marital relationship reaches the same conclusions held by our Christian tradition about marital intercourse. Psychologists tell us that sexual satisfaction does not depend on the physical performance as much as it depends on the emotional intimacy and the courage of spouses to be open and honest with each other.[19]

We also learn from the many books written by experts on human sexuality that many of the sexual problems experienced by spouses today are not the result of physical problems. Rather, they stem from the partners' inability to truly be intimate and fully give themselves to each other. The difficulties that many spouses experience in sexual intercourse cannot always be easily cured with a pill, as advertisers claim. Sexual problems are often caused by the emotional and spiritual gaps rooted in selfishness that exist between husband and wife. It is selfishness that keeps spouses from giving themselves to each other as a sincere gift.

As you read the chapters of this book you are walking the path of love traced for us by Jesus with his actions. The three qualities of love we learned from Jesus' example so far are: welcome and acceptance, the commitment to be present, and total self-giving, even to the point of painful sacrifices. These are the first three steps on the path of love and the blueprint for a happy marriage. Practicing these three steps leads you to transform your relationship into an interpersonal communion and to experience the happiness that your heart desires.

The next chapter will deal with the quality of love that repairs the relationship when it has been hurt by selfishness. The fourth step on the path of love is forgiveness.

▶ SIMPLE ACTS YOU CAN DO TODAY

1. Do something that you know your spouse appreciates and does not expect. Don't make a big deal about it. Just do it.

2. Find an opportunity to resolve one of your conflicts in a manner that is acceptable to both of you. For example, if your spouse disagrees with or does not like something you want, stop pushing your wishes and take time to listen to your spouse's feelings or point of view. Seek a compromise you both can live with.

3. When you notice that your spouse is doing or has done something for you, acknowledge his or her actions. Express your gratitude. Say "Thank you! I appreciate..." and state exactly what they have done.

4. In your prayers ask God to help you always to be mindful of doing what is good for your spouse, and doing this generously without expecting anything in return.

▶ LISTEN TO GOD'S STORY

The Annunciation—Mary submits to God's will: Luke 1:26–38
The Last Supper: Matthew 26:26–29
Jesus' death on the Cross: John 19:16–30

▶ REFLECT ON YOUR STORY

» Do you ever feel that your married life is a three-legged race? What situations come to mind when you think of it this way?

» As partners in a three-legged race are you and your spouse headed in the same direction? Are your priorities in life and your individual goals synchronized? Do you have a joint understanding about how to handle your finances? Do you have an agreement about children and the parenting style you want to use?

» Do you and your spouse agree on how you will make decisions together? Is it clear to both of you what kind of decisions each can make without consulting the other first?

» During your conflicts are you able to call a truce so that you do not let your emotions move you to say things you will regret? Discuss with your spouse how you can help each other keep your conflicts from escalating out of control.

» What are some of the situations in your daily routine that provide you with opportunities to be more generous toward your partner? Please list them.

» How do you stand up to your spouse when you are asked to do something you are not comfortable doing or that you think is wrong?

▶ ENDNOTES

1. *The Sacramentary.* New York: Catholic Book Publishing Co., 1985, p. 545.

2. "The sacred partnership of true marriage is constituted both by the will of God and the will of man. From God comes the very institution of marriage...while man, through generous surrender of his own person made to another for the whole span of life, becomes, the author of each particular marriage." Pius XI, *Casti Connubii, #9.*

3. *U.S. Census Bureau: Number, Timing, and Duration of Marriages and Divorces: 1996.* Washington, DC: Census Bureau Publications, February 2002.

4. Jung, Carl. *Man and His Symbols.* New York: Dell Publishing, 1968, pp. 125-27.

5. John Paul II. *Mulieris Dignitatem,* Washington, DC: United States Catholic Conference, 1988, #16.

6. "To the common good both man and woman make their specific contribution. Hence one can discover, at the very origins of human society, the qualities of communion and of complementarity." John Paul II, *Letter to Families*, #6.

7. "The author of the letter to the Ephesians sees no contradiction between an exhortation formulated in this way and the words: 'Wives, be subject to your husbands, as to the Lord. For the husband is the head of the wife' (5:22–23). The author knows that this way of speaking, so profoundly rooted in the customs and religious traditions of the time, is to be understood and carried out in a new way: As a 'mutual subjection out of reverence for Christ' (cf. Eph 5:21)." John Paul II, *Mulieris Dignitatem*, #24.

8. "Love causes man to find fulfillment through the sincere gift of self. To love means to give and to receive something which can be neither bought nor sold, but only given freely and mutually." John Paul II, *Letter to Families*, #11.

9. Benedict XVI. *Deus Caritas Est*. Washington, DC: United States Catholic Conference, 2005, #9.

10. Gottman and Silver, *The Seven Principles for Making Marriage Work*, p.15.

11. Dowrick, Stephanie. *Forgiveness and Other Acts of Love*. New York: W.W. Norton and Co., 1997, p. 200.

12. Welwood, John. *Journey of the Heart*. New York: Harper Perennial, 1990, p. 41.

13. Gottman and Silver, *The Seven Principles for Making Marriage Work*, p. 130.

14. Gottman and Silver, *The Seven Principles for Making Marriage Work*, p. 100.

15. "Consequently each man must look within himself to see whether she who was entrusted to him as a sister in humanity, as a spouse, has not become in his heart an object of adultery; to see whether she who, in different ways, is the co-subject of this existence in the world, has become for him an 'object': an object of pleasure, of exploitation." John Paul II, *Mulieris Dignitatem*, #14.

16. "Sexuality is a source of joy and pleasure: The Creator himself...established that in the (generative) function, spouses should experience pleasure and enjoyment of body and spirit. Therefore, the spouses do nothing evil in seeking this pleasure and enjoyment. They accept what the Creator has intended for them. At the same time, spouses should know how to keep themselves within the limits of just moderation [Pius XII, Discourse, October 29, 1951]." *Catechism of the Catholic Church*, #2362.

17. "For contrary to the superficial view of sex, according to which love (meaning here erotic love) culminates in a woman's surrender of her body to a man, we should rightly speak of the mutual surrender of both persons, of their belonging

equally to each other. Not mutual sexual exploitation so that each can obtain the maximum sexual pleasure, but the reciprocated gift of self, so that two persons belong each to the other." Wojtyla, Karol. *Love and Responsibility*. New York: Farrar-Straus-Giroux, 1981, p. 126.

18. "Uniting with each other (in the conjugal act) so closely as to become 'one flesh,' man and woman, rediscover, so to speak, every time and in a special way, the mystery of creation. They return in this way to that union in humanity ('bone of my bone and flesh of my flesh') which allows them to recognize each other and, like the first time, to call each other by name." John Paul II (General Audience, November 21, 1979). *Original Unity of Man and Woman: In the First Chapters of Genesis, Marriage Is One and Indissoluble.*

19. Brody, Steve, Ph. D., and Cathy Brody, M.S. *Renew Your Marriage at Midlife*. New York: Penguin Book, 1999, p. 187.

CHAPTER 8

I Forgive You and Ask for Forgiveness

Just as Christ forgives his bride, the church, through the sacrament of reconciliation, you are to forgive your spouse.

"God, the Father of mercies, through the death and resurrection of his Son has reconciled the world to himself and sent the Holy Spirit among us for the forgiveness of sins; through the ministry of the church may God give you pardon and peace, and I absolve you from your sins in the name of the Father, and of the Son, and of the Holy Spirit."

■ RITE OF RECONCILIATION[1]

Acouple came to my office in a great state of turmoil. It was during the Christmas season and all around was festive—but my counseling room was full of tension and gloom. The man and woman sitting in front of me were an image of pain, discomfort, and confusion. Marianne* spoke first. Pointing to her husband, Joe*, she said angrily to me: "I don't know if I can stay married to this man any longer. He is destroying our family. Last week, he went to Vegas, as he often does, for business. Well..." she paused, took a deep breath and then continued, tears streaming down her face, "he lost a fortune. He lost most of our savings." She paused again for a long time. Then, looking at her husband, she asked, "How can I live with someone who is a threat to my children's future and to mine? I have to protect my children and myself."

Joe's face was mournful and repentant. His eyes were tearing. He held his head down and didn't say anything for a long time. Finally, he murmured, "I am sorry, Marianne! I am so sorry!" He started sobbing. "Please forgive me. I know I made a terrible mistake. Thirty thousand dollars is a lot of money for our family, but I do not want to lose you and the children over it. I will do whatever is necessary to repair the damage and to regain your trust."

Unfortunately, serious situations like this one do happen, and when they do they cause great damage to the marriage and to the family. Relationships may be broken because of an addiction, an affair, a decision to do something knowing the spouse does not approve, or by a conscious act of keeping something from the spouse that he or she should know. These injuries to the relationship take place because of selfishness. One person chooses his or her wants over what is good for the spouse and the family. And thus, where there was union and love, there is now sadness and brokenness. The only way to repair the damage done by our selfish acts is reconciliation through forgiveness and reparation for the damage done.

Forgiveness is the subject of this chapter. The last three chapters introduced attitudes and behaviors that best express the qualities of true love: acceptance, presence, and self-giving. These are the attitudes that Adam and Eve had toward each other when God brought them together to be

*name has been changed

husband and wife. Acceptance, presence, and self-giving are the essential ingredients of any successful marital relationship. To the extent that these exist in your marriage, you will feel fulfillment and joy.

Unfortunately, in our daily life we struggle to accept each other, to be attentive, to be honest, and to be generous. We fail to love because we give in to selfishness. We criticize when we should try to understand, we lie when we should be honest, and we demand when we should be giving. In other words, we often hurt each other and our relationship. There is only one true cure for the pains we inflict on one another. It is forgiveness. To heal our emotional and spiritual wounds we need to be willing to acknowledge our failings and shortcomings, ask for forgiveness, and make reparation for the damage done.

George's* Story: I Acted Like a Spoiled Child

One late Sunday afternoon, Marcie* and I and our two young children sat down for dinner. It was a bright sunny day in early spring and I was hoping to go hit some golf balls after dinner. Marcie served the meal and we started eating. As I took the first few bites I noticed that the food did not taste as I expected it would. I saw that it was overcooked, and in fact some of it was burned. I tensed up and dropped my fork on the plate. I was annoyed and said to Marcie, "I work all week and slave for you guys and I cannot even have a decent meal on Sunday!" Marcie did not respond, so I turned toward her raising my voice: "If you didn't watch so much TV and talk so much on the phone with your friends you would have the time to cook a decent meal for us."

She replied softly: "I am sorry about the dinner!"

That was not good enough for me. Although a voice inside my mind was telling me to stop, I stood up, picked up the bottle of beer I was drinking, and threw it at the TV. At this point both children, ages five and seven, were in tears. The bottle hit the TV screen, which shattered with a big boom. I walked away from the table, picked up my golf clubs, and headed for the driving range. I peeled out of my driveway and sped up through the neighborhood. I was in a state of rage.

When I got home that evening I came face to face with another unpleasant reality. The TV, my friend, my escape in moments of stress, was gone. I had killed it in my fury. Watching TV was my way of forgetting my problems. Now my friend was not there for me. I had to deal, all by myself, with my feelings of guilt for my behavior toward my family and my disappointment with myself. Marcie was upstairs with the children. I truly was sorry. But I was too proud and stubborn to go up and admit it to Marcie. So, I sat in my chair just staring at the broken TV, in the dark.

Think about the last hurtful exchange you had with your spouse. It may have started with one person being late, or someone forgetting to do something, or simply a tone of voice that was misunderstood. Then, in reaction or retaliation, words intended to hurt were said by one of you. The other responded with counter-accusations and sarcastic remarks, and the two of you went back and forth trading ever more vicious insults. One of you may have decided to take the final stand in the growing conflict: You walked away and started the "silent treatment." Does this sound familiar to you?

According to the research done at the Seattle Marital and Family Institute, these skirmishes are a typical pattern in all marital relationships. Unfortunately, these battles can prove to be lethal to the marriage if you cannot stop them from escalating and if they happen often.

▶ THE FOUR HORSEMEN

The researchers of the Seattle Marital and Family Institute have identified four specific behaviors that lead spouses in a downward spiral of negative interactions. They are: criticism, contempt, defensiveness, and stonewalling. These have been called by Gottman's research team the "Four Horsemen of the Apocalypse"[2] because they are the harbingers of death to the marital relationship.

The First Horseman is criticism. Criticism is blaming one's spouse for something that has happened. Keep in mind that criticism is different from a complaint. A complaint or a disagreement can be stated in a respectful manner, that is, in a way that is not intended to hurt. Criticism, instead, contains the sting of condemnation that provokes the spouse, such as: "You never listen to me!" or "You always make us late!" The more habitual this behavior becomes, the more likely it is that this horseman will take up permanent residence and will invite the second one—contempt—to come into your relationship.

Contempt happens when a spouse insults the other knowing that this will cause pain to that person. For example, a spouse may say to the other with a sarcastic tone: "How stupid are you?" or "Only an idiot would do such a thing!" or "That's a dumb question!" Contempt is a form of abuse. Contemptuous remarks can be name-calling, sarcastic remarks, putdowns, rolling of the eyes, and gestures intended to demean the other person.

When contempt is present, defensiveness, the third horseman, follows closely behind. In fact, defensiveness is the counterattack of one spouse to the contemptuous remarks or criticism of the other. Then, as the mutual attacks escalate, one of the spouses will start stonewalling.

Stonewalling is the fourth horseman to make an appearance. It comes on the scene when one person intentionally chooses to ignore anything the other says or does the silent treatment. This behavior sends a message to the other that states: "Whatever you are saying is not worth listening or responding to! You are insignificant to me!"

The Four Horsemen get settled in the relationship through a cycle of negativity that progressively erodes the bond and destroys anything positive that exists in the marriage.

Can you relate to the image of the Four Horsemen? Some of these horsemen are likely to make an appearance in any relationship. Hopefully, they do not settle in. I am sure that you have witnessed their presence sometimes in other couples' relationships, and perhaps in yours. I once knew a husband and wife who let these horsemen completely take over their life. The spouses would go around with their swords drawn all the time. When he spoke, she would criticize him or discount his words with an endless litany of all of his inadequacies. He would wait for his turn to cut her down with equally vicious sarcastic remarks and putdowns. Eventually they did not speak to each other at all. This created a lot of pain not only for them but also for their children and friends. Needless to say, their marriage ended. They tore each other up, and let the hooves of their horses trample so much over each one's ego that nothing was left of the relationship. A sad situation!

▶ LEARNING TO BREAK THE PATTERN

Although these behaviors may be present in your relationship you can learn to stop the cycle of negativity and strengthen your marriage. Marriage therapists say that the secret weapon of the happy couple is the ability of the spouses to stop the fighting in order to restore peace to the relationship. They do so by responding to unpleasant incidents in their relationship with actions and words that defuse the tension rather than escalate it. They may say: "Sorry, I didn't mean to hurt you," or make a funny face, give a gentle touch, or tell a joke that expresses good will and changes the subject. Through simple words that convey regret or forgiveness they restore the harmony in their relationship. Happy couples learn to stop themselves before their arguments get out of control. Calling a "time out" to regain composure and rationality is a good way to keep from inflicting senseless wounds on each other. Think about your own interactions during a conflict. What do you or your spouse do to stop a negative exchange from getting out of control and escalating into a major battle?

"Repair attempts"[3] are important for the health of your relationship, but to succeed you need an attitude of forgiveness that can overlook a mistake your spouse made or a hurt inflicted unintentionally. Forgiveness plays a critical role in keeping your marital relationship healthy. Forgiveness is what prevents the Four Horsemen from settling in. The Four Horsemen hurt; forgiveness heals. The Four Horsemen divide; forgiveness reconnects.

▶ FORGIVENESS IS AN ATTITUDE

"Forgiveness is not an occasional act, it is a permanent attitude," said Martin Luther King, Jr.[4] Forgiveness must become a way of life for spouses who want to succeed in marriage. Forgiveness is an attitude founded on humility and realism, founded first of all on the humble acknowledgment that "I am not perfect and I am a sinner like anyone else." Jesus invites us to become aware of this when he challenged the Scribes and Pharisees who brought to him a woman caught in adultery to cast the first stone, if they had not sinned. Of course, they all recognized their sinfulness (Jn 8:3–11). The root of forgiveness in marriage is the realization that we are imperfect and that we too need to be forgiven.

▶ FORGIVENESS IS FOUNDED ON TRUTH

Forgiveness is also founded on realism. John Paul II writes: "Forgiveness... has its own intrinsic demands, the first of which is respect for the truth."[5] Forgiveness cannot come at the expense of ignoring problems. Forgiveness demands that the facts be acknowledged and that action be taken to keep them from happening again. It is through reparation and a change in behaviors that trust can be restored. Marianne, in the previous story of the gambler, could not forgive without also facing the damage caused to the family and to the relationship by her husband's actions. She realistically had to consider the risk of a possible recurrence. In a subsequent counseling session Marianne said to Joe, "What will you do to help me trust you again? You know, this was not the first time you squandered our money at a gambling table. Do you remember two summers ago? You lost all of our vacation money! And do you remember the previous summer? I am not a fool. It will take a long time for me to trust you again."

Joe made promises, but Marianne had to be realistic. For Marianne to forgive Joe meant being willing to live with the consequences of what Joe had done. She also had to protect herself and the family from future damage. She took over managing the family finances. Joe agreed to have limited access to the family money to protect the family from his gambling addiction.

Forgiveness is very difficult and often requires much courage. Reconciliation is based on reparation for the damage done and a promise to keep this from happening again.

▶ FORGIVENESS IS UNNATURAL

John Paul II writes: "Certainly, forgiveness does not come spontaneously or naturally to people. Forgiving from the heart can sometimes be heroic."[6]

Stephanie Dowrick says: "Forgiveness deeply offends the rational mind, when someone has offended us there is no reason why we should let that offense go."[7] Our instincts tell us that we should get even: "An eye for an eye and a tooth for a tooth" (Mt 5:38), but Jesus teaches us: Forgive if you want to be forgiven (Mt 6:12). If you do not forgive your spouse your relationship is destined to failure.

Forgiveness is more than "not getting even." To forgive means accepting the challenge of living with the consequences of what your spouse has done. It means letting go of the anger, the fear, the hurt, and the pain you feel. These negative emotions cloud everything in your relationship; and if you hang on to them they will damage or destroy it.

In an article published in *Marriage Partnership*[8] magazine a woman tells of her agony and humiliation when her husband was arrested for soliciting a prostitute. She tells how she and her husband struggled to put the pieces of their relationship back together. She points out that forgiveness for her meant putting the incident behind and moving on. Forgiveness meant not bringing the subject up over and over, for the sake of the relationship.

She wrote: "One day about four months later, when I brought up the subject again, Michael finally reached his breaking point. He said he loved me and he was truly sorry for what he'd done, but he couldn't live married to me any longer if I couldn't forgive and let go of what happened. I realized I was now destroying our marriage." The fact is that if a spouse chooses not to let go of the pain and move forward, the bitterness that he or she feels will poison the marriage and affect all aspects of their life together.

Forgiveness is not a sign of weakness; it is a way of distancing yourself from the pain you suffer because of what your spouse has done. Dowrick quotes the following words from the work of Dawna Markova: "(Forgiveness) is simply a movement to release and ease your heart of the pain and hatred that binds it. It is the harvested fruit of a season of darkness, followed by a season of growth, and very hard work."[9]

The hard work in the process of reconciliation and forgiveness begins by taking the first steps toward turning yourself back toward your spouse. In a moment of betrayal each spouse turns away from the other, out of self-defense. Reconciliation requires a turning back toward each other with a desire to move closer to your spouse. This is the first step toward restoring peace.

Recall the previous story of George and Marcie. The story points to the fact that it takes courage to ask for forgiveness as well as to forgive. It was difficult for George to face Marcie and it was difficult for Marcie to face George. Have you and your spouse been in a similar place of neither one wanting to make the first step toward the other? If you were in George's or Marcie's position what would you do to make the first step toward reconciliation? Would you be the first to turn toward the other and seek reconciliation, or would you wait for your spouse to take the first step? What would you do to break the ice?

▶ TAKING THE FIRST STEP

Whether you are the offender or the offended, I encourage you to always be the first to reach out to your spouse to seek reconciliation. This is the lesson about love we learn from God. In all cases of betrayal by Israel, his chosen people, God was always there to reach out to his people. He never turned his back on humankind, regardless of how sinful. This is well expressed in the Eucharistic Prayer the priest recites during the Mass: "Even when he [humankind] disobeyed you and lost your friendship, you did not abandon him to the power of death....Again and again you offered a covenant to man."[10] As followers of Jesus we are expected to reach out in forgiveness if we expect to be ourselves forgiven. This is what we pray each time we recite the Our Father: "And forgive us our debts, as we also have forgiven our debtors" (Mt 6:12). Christ himself gave us a heroic example of what it means to forgive. As he hung on the cross in agony he begged his Father: "Forgive them; for they do not know what they are doing" (Lk 23:34). He was forgiving and asking God's forgiveness for those who had turned against him and were killing him.

When Peter asked Jesus how many times a person should forgive, Jesus answered: Seventy times seven, which meant as many times as you are offended (Mt 18:21–22). St. Paul writes to the Colossians: "Bear with one another and, if anyone has a complaint against another, forgive each other; just as the Lord has forgiven you" (Col 3:13).

▶ FORGIVENESS IS A WORK OF GRACE

Forgiveness, like other virtues, is not easy because, when an injury has been committed, it breaks our trust and wounds our ego. Often, only time can bring full healing because behaviors must be changed and trust must be rebuilt. John Paul II reminds us that: "Forgiveness is the condition for reconciliation but this cannot take place without interior transformation and conversion—which is the work of grace."[11] To bring about the interior transformation, the change of heart required of both spouses, Christians have a powerful tool in their faith in God. Acknowledging one's need for God's help in prayer gives strength to the offender and to the offended, to open their hearts to each other, to make changes in the behavior that is the source of the pain, and to put the past behind.

To help us grow in our relationship through reconciliation, the Catholic Church offers us the sacrament of reconciliation. In this ritual Christ himself, through the words and actions of the priest, cleanses us from our sin, and reminds us that he stands by our side always ready to help us make the changes necessary for the good of the relationship. The *Catechism of the Catholic Church* teaches us that "Christ dwells with them [the spouses], gives them the strength to take up their crosses and to follow him, to rise again after they have fallen, to forgive one another, to bear one another's burdens, to be subject to one another with supernatural, tender, and fruitful love."[12]

Forgiveness is an act of love. In a marital relationship, forgiveness removes barriers and rebuilds bridges. It opens doors that were closed. It turns spouses back toward each other. It reconnects them and lets the life of the relationship flow again. When this happens, tension, anger, and hurt are released, healing takes place, the emotional life can blossom, and communion grows. Peace returns to the relationship because spouses have renewed their promise to be with each other and for each other, and happiness springs once more because husband and wife feel in their relationship the presence of God.

▶ SIMPLE ACTS YOU CAN DO TODAY

1. If your spouse does something that hurts you, let your spouse know. Ask your spouse not to do this again, and tell your spouse that you forgive him or her. Do not let time pass, hoping you will get over it and will feel different tomorrow.

2. When you do something that injures your spouse, ask your spouse for forgiveness. Say: "I am sorry for..." and state what you regret

having done or said, and promise not to repeat that again. Ignoring the incident and hoping your spouse will get over it is not conducive to your growth in love.

3. If you and your spouse get into an argument that seems to be escalating, be the first to take action to stop the escalation. Ask for a "time out" to think about your spouse's point of view.

4. In your prayers ask God to help you forgive your spouse and pray that your spouse can forgive your own faults.

▶ LISTEN TO GOD'S STORY

The woman caught in adultery: John 8:3–11
The prodigal son: Luke 15:11–31
The unforgiving servant: Matthew 18:23–35
The Our Father: Matthew 6:9–15

▶ REFLECT ON YOUR STORY

» Think about the story of Joe and Marianne. If you were in Marianne's position what would you do?

» When was the last time you saw or heard one of the Four Horsemen (criticism, contempt, defensiveness, and stonewalling) in your relationship?

» By what words and gestures do you recognize the presence of the Four Horsemen in your relationship?

» How do you and your spouse stop arguments from escalating into big battles? What are the "repair attempts" you and your spouse use effectively?

» Think of George's story. Do you ever find yourself in situations where you are unwilling to take the first step to ask for forgiveness? What keeps you from taking the first step?

» Has your relationship been tested with what you would consider major acts of betrayals? If yes, how have you been able to overcome these and turn back toward each other?

» Do you and your spouse pray for each other, especially when you find that you are hurting each other and pulling apart?

▶ ENDNOTES

1. *The Rites of the Catholic Church as Revised by the Second Vatican Ecumenical Council*, Study Edition, p. 383.

2. Gottman, John M., Ph.D., *Why Marriages Succeed or Fail*, p. 68.

3. "This name refers to any statement or action—silly or otherwise—that prevents negativity from escalating out of control. Repair attempts are the secret weapon of emotionally intelligent couples." Gottman and Silver, *The Seven Principles for Making Marriage Work*, p. 22.

4. Setzer, Claudia. *Quotable Soul*. New York: John Wiley & Sons, 1994, p. 91.

5. John Paul II, edited by Joseph Durepos. *Go in Peace*. Chicago: Loyola Press, 2003, p. 29.

6. John Paul II, *Go in Peace*, p. 28.

7. Dowrich, Stephanie, *Forgiveness and Other Acts of Love*, p. 291.

8. Arlene, Amber. *Marriage Partnership*, Spring 2003, Vol. 20, No.1, p. 58.

9. Dowrich, Stephanie, *Forgiveness and Other Acts of Love*, p. 293.

10. Roman Missal, Eucharistic Prayer IV.

11. John Paul II, *Go in Peace*, p. 30.

12. *Catechism of the Catholic Church*, #1642.

CHAPTER 9

Comfort and Help Each Other Heal

Just as Christ heals and comforts his bride, the church, you are to comfort and help your spouse heal.

"Make this oil a remedy for all who are anointed with it; heal them in body, in soul, and in spirit, and deliver them from every affliction."

■ RITE OF ANOINTING OF THE SICK[1]

"Love and intimacy are among the most powerful factors in health and illness." ■ Dr. Dean Ornish[2]

▶ A DARK HOUR

Love heals in many ways, and marital love is a great source of strength and courage during difficult moments in life. I still remember vividly one of the saddest days of my life. It was December 6, 1995, the feast of St. Nicholas. During the afternoon, my manager called me into her office and told me that my job had been eliminated. The company was downsizing. My services, my skills, and I were found to be superfluous. (There are many employees and workers in America today who have had a similar humiliating experience.)

That day is etched in my memory, not only because of the personal put-down I felt after eight years of service to my employer, but also because of the trauma that it caused my whole family. As I walked out of the meeting with my manager, I was in a daze. All I could think about was what effect this would have on my family. We lived in a comfortable neighborhood, surrounded by good friends. Laura, our youngest, attended a private school that she loved. Teri had a job that she found very rewarding at our parish church. I thought to myself: "Our dream will be shattered. We will lose all of this." I felt very sad.

In the midst of sadness, I remembered that Teri, at that very moment, was picking Laura up from school and taking her to the orthodontist to start her treatment with braces. I immediately thought: "Perhaps we should wait on the braces. We may have to move. In a few weeks, we will lose our family dental coverage. After that, my severance will run out. Our future is uncertain." With a broken heart, I called Teri at the orthodontist's office. Teri told the doctor what had happened. Together, we all decided to postpone the start of this treatment. This was especially traumatic for Laura, who was already sitting in the orthodontist's chair.

At home, that evening I felt my family's love most fully. I knew that Teri and Laura were in pain. They were just as scared, angry, and confused as I was. However, they did not show that to me. All I saw in them was their concern for me. I was distraught and cried a lot. I knew that our life would change and everyone in our family would be negatively affected by this event. I felt responsible for all the pain my family would experience. Teri did not ask many questions. She just held me and caressed my forehead. Her quiet and courageous presence of concern for me told me of her love and gave me the strength to put my hurts and anger aside and move on.

I was able to bounce back very quickly from the shock and the hurt because of Teri's and Laura's care and love. Within hours, I started an extensive job search. In fact, the next morning I called local employers, seeking job opportunities. This lasted for almost six months. During this time I felt continuous love and support from Teri and my family. These were difficult days for everyone. However, the love we felt for one another was a real blessing. It was a great source of strength for all of us during this difficult moment in our lives.

▶ SUFFERING—OUR INHERITANCE

When physical illnesses or emotional sufferings touch us, we come face to face with our own limitations and mortality. Such experience of vulnerability is another aspect of the inheritance our progenitors, Adam and Eve, passed down to us. You may recall what God said to Adam and Eve before sending them out of the Garden of Eden. God spoke to the primordial woman and said, "In pain you shall bring forth children" (Gen 3:16), and God said to Adam, "By the sweat of your face you shall eat bread until you return to the ground, for out of it you were taken; you are dust, and to dust you shall return" (Gen 3:19). With these words the human race was condemned not only to toil but also to die.

Death, sickness, anxiety, pain, fatigue, and many of the unpleasant experiences we encounter today are part of our human condition. When we are sick or upset we feel vulnerable and alone. We depend on others to help us overcome our limitations and shortcomings. The process of healing is generally a relational one. Throughout history human beings have recognized the role that others play in their healing process. They have identified healers among them: shamans, medicine men, priests, faith healers, nurses, psychologists, doctors, and others.

▶ HUSBAND AND WIFE ARE EACH OTHER'S HEALERS

In marriage, husbands and wives become each other's primary comforters and healers, not only physically, but also spiritually. The Catholic Church expresses this in many of her teachings. The bishops gathered at the Second Vatican Council in Rome stated that God has given marital love many gifts, among these are the power to heal and to help the spouses perfect each other.[3]

Do you remember the last time you were sick or upset? Was it comforting for you to have your spouse near you and help you with your needs? Do you remember the last time you received valuable advice, encouragement, or even nagging from your spouse?

Yes, even spousal nagging is beneficial, say researchers. Linda Waite, a professor of sociology at the University of Chicago, and Maggie Gallagher, a nationally syndicated columnist, write that men benefit from the support of their wives' persuasive insistence. "A spouse's nagging can have a powerful impact on one's health for both men and women, but more so for men."[4] And Waite adds: "A wife feels licensed to nag in a way that a girlfriend does not, precisely because both the wife and her husband know their lives are intertwined."[5]

Similarly, an article published in *50+Health*[6] states that men become health conscious and benefit greatly under the pressure of their spouse. Denise Knowles reports in this same article that men are reluctant to get physical exams because of an almost inbred belief in their own "invincibility." According to this article, a survey conducted by Market and Opinion Research International found that eighty percent of males visiting a doctor did so because their spouse suggested it. These findings resonated with me. Years ago, upon returning from a business trip to Singapore, during the Severe Acute Respiratory Syndrome (SARS) epidemic, I caught a cold that made me very congested. Teri insisted that I see our family doctor to whom I declared, "I am here because Teri made me come." He smiled and commented, "You must always listen to your wife. She's looking out for your best interest." Luckily, he proclaimed me free of SARS.

▶ THE POSITIVE POWER OF THE MARITAL RELATIONSHIP

Researchers tell us that because of the love and care spouses give each other in marriage, those who are married fare much better in our society than those who are not. Again, Waite and Gallagher, in their book *The Case for Marriage*, point out that married people, because of what they do for each other, are healthier, happier, and better off financially. Here are some key points from their research.

Married people live longer. Married people have a lower mortality rate than those who are not married. Unmarried women have a mortality rate that is fifty percent higher than those who are married. Unmarried men have a rate that is two-hundred-fifty percent higher than those who are married.[7] Researchers tell us that being married lengthens a man's life by an average of ten years.

Married people feel healthier. In self-rating on how healthy a person feels, both married men and women are thirty percent more likely to say that their health is excellent or very good than their counterparts who are single.

Married people are healthier physically. Getting married improves a person's general health. Self-disclosure has been proven to benefit physical and mental health. According to Waite, the self-disclosure forged in the marriage bed and over the kitchen table can actually help couples ward off physical illness. She also writes that married men and women are less likely than singles to suffer from long-term chronic illnesses or disabilities.

Married people enjoy better mental health. Married men and women report less depression, less anxiety, and lower levels of other types of psychological distress than those who are single, divorced, or widowed. Married men are only half as likely as bachelors, and about one-third as likely as divorced men, to take their own life.

Married people are happier. According to a study of 14,000 adults over a ten-year period, marital status is an important predictor of happiness. Forty percent of the married said they were very happy with their life in general, compared to fifteen percent of the separated and eighteen percent of the divorced.

Married people enjoy sex more. Married people have both more and better sex than singles do. They have sex more often and enjoy it more, both physically and emotionally, than the unmarried.

Married people are more productive and earn more. When it comes to building wealth or avoiding poverty, a stable marriage may be the most important asset. Both men and women are financially better off because they marry. Men earn more and women have access to more of men's earnings.

You benefit emotionally, physically, and financially from the love of your spouse because no one cares more about you and your health than your spouse. Your spouse's life and yours are grafted together and therefore are interdependent. Your health, your happiness, your financial success affect not only you but also your spouse and your children. Spouses protect each other; they help each other for their common good, they sacrifice for each other because they love each other. When difficulties arise they pull together and become interested in resolving the problems because one person's problem is a common problem that affects the whole family.

Spouses care not only about each other's physical health but also about one another's spiritual well-being. They encourage each other to go to church. They pray for each other and, as they grow in their spiritual life, they learn to pray together for their common blessings, their hopes and concerns. Caring for each other improves the quality of the relationship and leads to happiness.

Researchers find that the quality of the relationship is also an important factor in the healing process. Waite writes that the better the quality of the marital relationship, the better the health and the happiness of the spouses.[8] Conversely, researchers tell us that a couple's inability to resolve conflicts in a constructive manner can threaten their well-being.

Health experts say that positive interactions between spouses can boost the immune system and keep both partners healthy.[9] In other words, loving each other is good for you in every way. It is obvious that spouses tend to naturally comfort and help each other heal for their own self-preservation. However, comforting each other and helping each other heal is something spouses need to do out of love. Christ's love for the church is our model.

▶ CHRIST IS OUR MODEL

When Jesus walked the streets of Galilee and Judea he often encountered people in need of both spiritual and physical healing. Jesus manifested God's love and compassion for our wounded humanity by reaching out to them. Jesus healed through words and touch.

When Jesus healed the leper, the evangelist writes, "Jesus stretched out his hand and touched him, and said to him, 'Be made clean!' Immediately the leprosy left him" (Mk 1:41–42). Consider the example of the healing of the deaf mute. While Jesus was traveling the area near the Sea of Galilee the people brought to him a man who was deaf and had a speech impediment. He begged Jesus to heal him. Jesus took the man aside, away from the crowd. He put his fingers into his ears and spat on his own hand and touched the man's tongue. He looked up to heaven and said to the man "Ephphatha," which means, "Be opened!" The man's ears were opened, his tongue released, and he spoke (Mk 7:31–37).

Today, in the sacrament of anointing of the sick, Christ, through the words and actions of the priest, continues to heal and comfort his bride, the church. During the celebration of this rite the priest blesses the oil with the words: "Make this oil a remedy for all who are anointed with it; heal them in body, in soul, and in spirit, and deliver them from every affliction." Using the oil the priest anoints the forehead of the sick person saying: "Through this holy anointing may the Lord in his love and mercy help you with the grace of the Holy Spirit."[10]

Yesterday and today the power of God's love and mercy is manifested in Jesus' healing, which happened through touch and through words. In our daily life we express our love for our spouse through the same means. Through them, like Christ, we can bring comfort and healing to our beloved.

▶ THE POWER OF TOUCH

Michelangelo has immortalized the significance of touch as a life-giving act in the famous scene he painted on the ceiling of the Sistine Chapel in Rome. The creation of Adam is portrayed with the image of the hand of God reaching out to touch the hand of man. This touch makes Adam come to life. Touch has the power to nurture spouses physically, emotionally, and spiritually. It makes us feel connected to each other and it strengthens our intimacy. Touch soothes and energizes because it sends messages of care and love to the person who receives it.

Jesus healed with touch. He laid hands on sick people, he took them by the hand, he touched parts of their body. When Jesus healed Peter's mother-in-law "He touched her hand, and the fever left her" (Mt 8:15). When he healed the synagogue leader's daughter, the Gospel writer tells us: "He went in and took her by the hand, and the girl sat up" (Mt 9:23–26).

What spouses yearn to receive from each other more than anything else, in times of pain and stress, is support, which is often expressed with touch. In his book *The Five Love Languages*, Gary Chapman writes, "For some individuals, physical touch is their primary love language. Without it, they feel unloved."[11] I know from personal experience how important touch is to Teri. When she feels tired, stressed, or has a headache, there is no better remedy for her than having me massage her neck, her head, or her back.

Is your spouse a person who cherishes physical contact and benefits from your touch? If so, make a special effort to express your love in this fashion. If you are a person who does not feel a strong personal need for physical touch, you may want to make an effort to remember that your spouse, un-like you, may cherish being touched.

▶ WORDS THAT HEAL

Jesus used his words to heal. Throughout the Gospels we have examples of words that heal. To the Canaanite woman who came to ask Jesus to free her daughter from demons, he said: "'Woman, great is your faith! Be it done for you as you wish.' And her daughter was healed instantly" (Mt 15:21–28). Jesus spoke to the spirits possessing the epileptic boy brought to him by his father: "You spirit that keeps this boy from speaking and hearing, I command you, come out of him, and never enter him again" (Mk 9:25). To the paralytic that was brought to him on a bed he said: "I say to you, stand up and take your bed and go to your home" (Lk 5:24). The man stood up and went home.

Words are another means through which you reach out to your spouse to give encouragement, to praise, to compliment, and to give advice. The words you use and the tone of voice with which you deliver them affect your spouse. With your words you can hurt and you can heal.

In the book mentioned above, Gary Chapman also identifies words of affirmation as important. Words of affirmation are words that have a positive effect on the spouse. The book of Proverbs in the Bible expresses this thought well: "Anxiety weighs down the human heart, but a good word cheers it up" (12:25).

Listen to yourself and how you speak to your spouse. Think about how you use your words. Do you use them to praise, to encourage, to comfort and build up your spouse, or do you use them to criticize and to put down? How often do you compliment your spouse? Do you tell him or her that you appreciate what they do for you and for the family? Do you remark favorably on what he or she wears? If words of affirmation are not in your vocabulary today, learn to use them. Start by noticing what your spouse does for the family and for you, and comment on it in a positive way. As you do this be specific. For example: "I appreciate your help with dinner. The salad you made was very delicious."

On the same topic of using words to make each other better, think about how you give advice to your spouse. We all have our blind spots. It is our role as spouses to observe each other and tell what we see. Often our advice is difficult for our spouse to receive because of the way we deliver it. We may mean well, but what we say may be perceived as a putdown, a threat, or as patronizing. To be effective in giving your advice you need to practice humility. You need to put your thoughts on the table for your spouse to observe, hold out a mirror to your spouse, and let him or her decide what to do about what you observe. Do not be offended if he or she chooses not to follow your advice.

Talk to your spouse as a partner and not as a parent. Be a lover, not a tyrant. Listen to the tone of your voice. Understand how your words come across to your spouse. If you notice that your tone is not a loving one, adjust your voice so that your words can truly be an expression of love. I have learned from my spouse the importance of the tone of voice I use. Teri often asks me: "Do you hear yourself? It's your tone!" She's right, there are times when my tone does not match what my words are saying, and she can tell. Often the words I say are positive but the tone is demeaning, and all she hears is the negative.

Much more can be said about the use of touch and the use of words to give each other support and to heal each other's pains. What is important for every couple to remember is the example of Jesus. Whatever you do, do it for the right reason. Do it to heal, and to truly comfort. Make your words and actions a true gift of yourself to your spouse as Jesus did during his life on earth and continues to do today for his bride the church through the sacraments, especially the sacrament of anointing of the sick. You are your spouse's best healer.

▶ SIMPLE ACTS YOU CAN DO TODAY

1. Find an opportunity to hold your spouse's hand. It speaks volumes

without a word being said. It may happen when you go for a walk, when you watch TV, or in the car.

2. If your spouse enjoys physical touch, find at least one opportunity today to give the loving touch that he or she craves: a kiss, a hug, a rubbing of shoulders, a back massage, etc.

3. Find a way to give your spouse at least one compliment today. Use words that affirm the good you see in him or her.

4. Today, when your spouse makes a suggestion or gives you some advice, do not interrupt. Listen attentively and let your spouse finish making his or her point.

▶ LISTEN TO GOD'S STORY

How God loves us: Isaiah 66:13
Healing of the paralytic: Luke 5:17–26
Healing of the man with a withered hand: Matthew 12:9–14
Healing of the deaf mute: Mark 7:31–37

▶ REFLECT ON YOUR STORY

» Think of a time your spouse helped you feel better, whether physically or emotionally. What did he or she do?

» Reflect on your use of words that heal and affirm. How often do you compliment your spouse's good qualities and successes? On balance, do you criticize more often than affirm? If so, what can you do to reverse this pattern?

» Is it easy for you to receive advice from your spouse? If not, is it due to the fact that you resist advice, or is it the way the advice is delivered? If it is because of the way the advice is delivered, talk to your spouse about this. Your spouse's advice is important to you and it is in your best interest to hear it.

» Reflect on how important it is for you and for your spouse to be physically close to each other. Perhaps each of you has different needs for touch. Such needs should be addressed.

» Do you feel free and comfortable enough with your spouse to ask for a hug when you need one?

▶ ENDNOTES

1. *The Rites of the Catholic Church as Revised by the Second Vatican Ecumenical Council*, Study Edition, p. 656. Just before administering the anointing of the sick, the priest prays: "God of all consolation,...send the power of your Holy Spirit, the Consoler, into this precious oil, this soothing ointment." Then, during the anointing the priest says: "Make this oil a remedy for all who are anointed with it; heal them in body, in soul, and in spirit, and deliver them from every affliction."

2. Ornish, Dean, M.D. *Love and Survival*. New York: HarperCollins, 1997, p. 2.

3. "This love the Lord has judged worthy of special gifts, healing, perfecting, and exalting gifts of grace and charity." Abbott, *Documents of Vatican II, The Pastoral Constitution on the Church in the Modern World*, #48.
    Also: "Finally, let the spouses themselves...be joined to one another in equal affection, harmony of mind, and the work of mutual sanctification." Abbott, *Documents of Vatican II, The Pastoral Constitution on the Church in the Modern World*, #51.

4. Waite, Linda J. and Maggie Gallagher. *The Case for Marriage*. New York: Doubleday, 2000, p. 56.

5. Waite and Gallagher, *The Case for Marriag*, p. 62.

6. 50+Health, "For Better or Worse—Marriage and Health," www.50plushealth.co.uk.

7. Waite and Gallagher, *The Case for Marriag*, p. 50.

8. Waite and Gallagher, *The Case for Marriage*, p. 56.

9. WebMD, "The 'Language of Love' Good for Marriage—and Health." www.webmd.com.

10. *The Rites of the Catholic Church as Revised by the Second Vatican Ecumenical Council; Pastoral Care of the Sick*, #123 and #124.

11. Chapman, Gary. *The Five Love Languages*. Chicago: Northfield Publishing, 1995, p. 104.

CHAPTER 10

I Am at Your Service

Just as Christ serves his bride, the church, you are to serve your spouse and your family.

"Will you accept children lovingly from God, and bring them up according to the law of Christ and his church?"

■ THE WEDDING RITE[1]

S ervice is an activity that fulfills our human need to share with others our God-given goodness and our gifts. Serving others is an act of love that gives joy and connects us with one another. Service is one of the hallmarks of Christian life. At the Last Supper Jesus washed his disciples' feet and said, "The greatest among you must become like the youngest, and the leader like the one who serves....I am among you as one who serves"

(Lk 22:26–27). Peter in writing to the early Christians wrote, "Serve one another with whatever gift each of you has received" (1 Pet 4:10).

Albert Schweitzer wrote: "The only ones among you who will be really happy are those who will have sought and found how to serve."[2] It is said that the famous psychiatrist, Dr. Karl Menninger was once asked what advice he would give a person who feels the onset of a nervous breakdown. He replied that this person should lock up one's own house, go help someone in need. When we share our talents with others we affirm our giftedness, and we feel good.

Service helps us survive as a species, writes Dr. Dean Ornish.[3] When we serve one another we celebrate our humanity and acknowledge our interdependence. In service, we share our abundance to fill the needs of others; they share their scarcity to fill our abundant need for them. This is the essence of community. Communities cannot live and prosper without people willing to serve people. This applies also to the community of the family and to the relationship of husband and wife. Your marriage cannot survive without you and your spouse being willing to serve each other.

Think about how your spouse serves you daily. Gary Chapman, the author of *The Five Love Languages*,[4] writes that spouses serve each other when they cook meals, set the table, wash the dishes, clean the commode, get hair out of the sink, get the bugs off the windshield, take out the garbage, keep the car in operating condition, clean the garage, mow the grass, and many other household activities. All of these are acts of service. They are acts of love that are necessary to build the marital relationship. However, the service a married couple is called to provide is greater than just serving each other.

▶ GOD'S CALL TO SERVE

When God created the first couple, he did not create them to just be each other's best friends and companions. He created them to be each other's helpmates in tending to his creation, and he said to them: "Be fruitful and multiply, and fill the earth and subdue it" (Gen 1:28). In marriage spouses are called to follow God's command. As a couple they are called to build up society in their role as parents: "Be fruitful." As individuals they are called to tend to God's creation, to "subdue the earth" through their daily work.

Parenthood and work are two important ways in which a married couple serves God. And yet, these are also the sources of most conflicts and strife between spouses. Daily, both your children and your employers make high demands on you for time, energy, attention, and commitment. Because of this, you often can feel pulled in opposite directions, and frequently can neglect one in favor of the other. To succeed in managing the conflicts and the stresses produced by the demands of parenthood and the expectations of your job, you need to agree on your priorities.

Mark* and Judy*, the parents of two young children, were expecting their third child and were concerned about how their career-oriented lifestyle might impact the children. Judy said:

> We both work full time. We are professionals who work long hours each day. We do not mind the hours because we like the work we do and the money we make, but recently, with the new pregnancy we have been asking ourselves, "Why do we do this? Is this good for the children?"
>
> At 7 AM each day, on the way to work one of us drops off Jody, who is two, and Felicia, who is four, at daycare. The other picks them up at 6 PM in the evening. We rush home to cook dinner, one of us gives baths while the other cleans, then we all collapse from exhaustion. The next morning the merry-go-round starts over again.

Mark, who had been silently nodding in agreement, added, "We do not like the stress that our lifestyle creates in our home. To make matters worse, we often are so tired that Judy and I snap at each other or at the children, and that makes everyone feel very tense. Now that we are expecting our third child we feel it is time to reassess our priorities and consider our options. "

*name has been changed

Mark and Judy are typical young parents who are trying to balance making a living, pursuing careers, and caring for their children. This sorting of priorities is very challenging for young spouses, especially today.

Separating wants from needs and creating priorities that match our obligations is where the challenge resides.

▶ MARY AND JOSEPH

In counseling couples I have observed that a person's Christian faith can be of great help in remembering what is most important. Religious faith allows spouses to rise above their immediate desires and to remember that their relationship is foremost a call to serve God. Mary and Joseph, the parents of Jesus, are a perfect example of a couple that lived their lives aware of God's call to serve him.

Have you ever wondered what life was like in the home of Mary and Joseph during their days together in Nazareth? It is difficult to imagine their marital relationship because little has been written about them as a couple in the Gospels. However, from the sacred writers we learn one important quality of their relationship: They lived their life with the intent of serving God and each other in everything they did. They truly must have been *with* and *for* each other, united in their desire to serve God.

We see this quality in Mary who, when presented by the angel Gabriel with the mystery of her conception, said humbly: "Here am I, the servant of the Lord; let it be with me according to your word" (Lk 1:38). She put her life at the full disposal of God.

A similar attitude of service to God and care for Mary is visible in Joseph's decision to marry Mary. The evangelist Matthew tells us that, because Joseph cared about Mary, when he realized she was pregnant, he decided to break up their engagement so as not to cause her shame. However, when the angel explained to him the mystery of Mary's pregnancy, he too put his life at the full disposal of God and dedicated himself to serving God by choosing to make a home for Mary and her child (Mt 1:18–25).

When Herod threatened the infant Jesus' life, we see again Joseph's dedication to serve God and his family. Following the angel's command Joseph took Jesus and Mary to Egypt and the family stayed there until the danger was past. This was not easy for Joseph, who had to abandon his business in Nazareth, move to a foreign country, and start his business there to support his family.

Mary and Joseph's role as parents of Jesus was not an easy one. Consider what happened the day when Jesus strayed from the clan without telling his parents. Luke tells us that when Jesus was twelve his parents went to Jerusalem as they did each year to celebrate Passover. As Mary and Joseph were returning home after the celebrations they realized that Jesus was nowhere to be found among the members of their clan. Imagine how they felt. They frantically returned to Jerusalem to look for him. It took them three days to find him. Mary and Joseph had been afraid for his safety and upon finding him they were probably quite angry. Mary tells Jesus: "Child, why have you treated us like this? Look, your father and I have been searching for you in great anxiety" (Lk 2:48).

▶ THE CALL TO WELCOME AND TO NURTURE LIFE

Life as a married couple is not intended to be self-serving. John Paul II explains that the unity of husband and wife "rather than closing them up in themselves, opens them toward new life, toward a new person."[5] Husband and wife marry to become active partners with God to create and to nurture human life. On your wedding day the priest asked you: "Will you accept children lovingly from God and bring them up according to the law of Christ and his church?"[6] In responding "Yes" to this important question you agreed to let your love for each other be fruitful. Parenthood is an act of love and an act of service to God, to society, and to the children.

▶ TO BE A GOOD PARENT

Every parent wants to be a good parent, but that does not mean they need to be their children's maid or chauffeur, or personal waiter. However, that's how many parents feel today. If you find that your life is defined by your children's excessive activities, if you feel that you have to be at your children's disposal 24/7, then maybe you are acting more like a maid, a chauffeur, or a waiter than a parent. Is this what serving God and your children means? The answer is "No."

Often it is easier to give in to a child's demands than to resist and to say "no," or to pause and to explain. It is easier to pick up a messy room yourself or to do a task that should have been done by the child than to argue, prod, and hold a child accountable. It is easier to overlook infractions or uncivilized behaviors than to correct and to enforce the rules. Sometimes it is more expedient to act as a servant than as a parent. However, what your children need is a parent who truly cares by teaching them to be responsible, and not someone who waits on them. The true servant role of a parent is one of leader and educator.

A parent is a person put there by God to help the child be formed into a mature human being. A parent is a child's visible "guardian angel." Your role as a parent is to teach your children how to be humans for their own good, and the good of society. This means defining boundaries appropriate for a child's age, guiding with your advice and example, correcting, praising, enforcing the rules, expressing love, giving support and encouragement, and providing for your children's physical and spiritual needs.

Leading your children to become healthy, capable, and responsible citizens in your community is an awesome and wonderful responsibility. It is one that cannot ever be fully delegated to another person or institution. The Catholic Church teaches that the family is the first and fundamental school of social living.[7] Parents are the primary teachers of the social skills their children need to be good citizens.[8] The task of teaching children social skills and respect for the rules and the laws is very taxing; every parent should get a medal for such service. Some parents deserve a "Purple Heart" for the wounds suffered while parenting.

▶ THE IMPORTANCE OF THE MARITAL BOND

Parenthood is very demanding and requires commitment. But it is important that you do not let your dedication to your children be so totally consuming that it undermines the marital relationship. The marital relationship is the foundation of the family. It is the core relationship that precedes the advent of the children, and on which the children rely for stability and security, writes Dr. William Doherty in *Take Back Your Marriage*.[9]

What is most important to the children, especially during the formative years, is to be welcomed by their parents and to be embraced by them in their communion of love. It is in the parent's love for each other and for the child that the young person experiences love. Children feel love in their parents' acceptance, their constant presence, their sacrifices, their forgiveness for one's mistakes, their healing touch, and their constant care. It is in this loving embrace that children experience the feeling of "home," the place where they belong because they feel a part of it, and feel intimately connected to it. There they feel secure and loved. It is in this "home" that the child first experiences God's love, the matrix of our loving.

When this experience of marital communion is missing in a family great damage is done to the child, even if the parents choose to stay together. This is a fact that has been studied for many years and proven again and again by researchers. Consider the following statistics from the study *The Effect of Divorce on America* published by the Heritage Foundation in 2003.[10]

Children whose parents have divorced exhibit more health, behavioral, and emotional problems. They are involved more frequently in crime and drug abuse, and have a higher rate of suicide.

Children of divorced parents perform more poorly in reading, spelling, and math. They are also more likely to repeat a grade and to have higher dropout rates and lower rates of college graduation.

Similar findings come from Judy Wallerstein, who in her book, *The Un-expected Legacy of Divorce: A Twenty-Five-Year Landmark Study*, contends that divorce marks offspring for life. She finds that by the time children of divorced parents reach their thirties, only half of them are doing well in their personal lives. She says: "They come to adulthood burdened, frightened and worried about failure. They want love. They want commitment. They want what everybody else wants. But they're very afraid they'll never get it."[11] Elisabeth Marquardt comes to similar conclusions in her study on the lives of children of divorce published in a book called *Between Two Worlds: The Inner Lives of Children of Divorce*.[12]

For Catholics divorce and remarriage is not an option because we know from the Bible that no one can separate what God has joined in marriage (Mt 19:6).[13] However, we live in and are influenced by a secular and con-sumer culture that believes if you do not find your bliss in marriage, you are justified to seek a divorce. This attitude creates temptations we must resist at all costs.

If you know someone who is unhappy in their marriage, or may be struggling yourself, consider this: Researchers have found that those who divorced because they were unhappy were not any happier after the di-vorce. On the other hand, two-thirds of those who were unhappy and chose to stay together to work on the relationship described themselves as happy after five years.[14] Finally, consider the impact of divorce on chil-dren as mentioned above. Your children are better off in an intact loving family.

▶ WATCH YOUR CHILDREN GROW

Parents help their children grow through many personal sacrifices. They launch them into the world, watching with trepidation and prayer as they carry on the parents' legacy. There is nothing more awe-inspiring for a cou-ple than the sight of their own children growing up and doing a good job at raising their own families.

Carol, age sixty-five, is a vivacious woman. She is a grandmother who watches closely over the growth of her family. What she sees lifts her spirit to God in praise and thanksgiving. One evening, I had the privilege of listening to Carol share her experiences as a parent, as a grandparent, and as a spouse.

> Recently, Mickey, my husband, and I were visited by our oldest, Jim, who is thirty-five. He had just been at an interview for a job and was well dressed. He stood there in our living room in his suit, and was telling us about his interview and his hopes. As I looked at him I was taken by his energy and enthusiasm, his confidence in himself and his dreams. I listened to him attentively but images were flashing in my mind. I was recalling different incidents from his life as a child, then as a teenager and as a young man. I was feeling very proud. Moved by those feelings, I thanked God for Jim, for the person that he is. Looking at my children growing up and raising their own families I cannot help but turn to God and be thankful. As grandparents we feel very close to God.

Mickey, Carol's husband, who is a permanent deacon at our parish and helps parents prepare for the baptism of their children, shares with the new parents the following anecdote about his own efforts to instill the Christian faith in his children.

> As a young parent, I was taught to bless my children each evening after their night prayers. I did so by raising my right hand and solemnly tracing a cross in the air over each of them, like the priest does when he blesses the people at the end of Mass. The ritual would end with a little pinch on their nose as a signal to them that the day was done.
>
> One evening, when Jim, my oldest, was twelve he looked up at me after the pinch on the nose and said, "Dad I don't need your blessing any more." Mike, who was just a few years younger, took

the opportunity of chiming in, "Yea, Dad, and I don't need it either." I was disappointed but I understood. Jim was stepping into a new world and did not want this open religious display from his father. Although I stopped making the sign of the cross over them, I did not stop blessing them. I told them that whenever I said good night to them that was my blessing for each of them.

Years passed and Jim went off to college and Mike went to Knoxville as a photojournalist with Channel 10. Later, Jim decided to join the Marines. The day he left for Officer Candidate School, we were at the airport waiting for his plane to leave. Jim turned to me and said: "Dad, would you give me your blessing?" I knew what he meant and gladly obliged.

Today, I know that both Jim and Mike bless their children, like I used to bless them and I am confident that one day, in a moment of need, I will ask them to bless me.

We parents cannot be shy about our faith with our children. They need us to share it with them and to practice it with them. They need us to help them form those religious habits, such as praying regularly and attending Mass each Sunday that will sustain them for the rest of their life. While there may be times when they question the faith and religious practices you instilled in them, and may even distance themselves from them, the examples of devotion and practice witnessed in you will never be forgotten and will remain a significant point of reference in their life.

▶ CHILDREN DO NOT ALWAYS FOLLOW THE PATH

Parents feel successful when they observe the success of their children. However, parents are not failures if their children do not develop as they had hoped. Children, especially adult sons and daughters, are individuals who make their own choices independent of what they learned from their parents. Sometimes these choices are contrary to what their parents would wish.

▶ TOUGH LOVE

Donna* came to work one morning and said to me:

> You would never believe what Rick* and I had to do last night. You know that we have been having a lot of problems with Benny*. He is seventeen and he has become very rebellious. He skips school, stays out late in the evenings, likes parties where there is drinking and smoking. If we ground him he finds a way to sneak out. I get very angry when I realize that we have lost control over him. Recently, the family counselor introduced us to a group of parents who have similar problems and they meet regularly to help one another. Their philosophy is called "Tough Love." According to them, we should not put up with Benny's behavior. So, we told Benny that the next time he came home past a curfew his bags would be packed and we would take him to another family's home who has agreed to take him. We also told him that if we found out that he was drinking we would take him immediately to an alcohol rehabilitation center.
>
> Last night Benny came home three hours past his curfew and his breath was reeking with alcohol. We had no choice. At two o'clock this morning we admitted him to the rehabilitation center. You don't know how much it hurts to turn your son over to someone else because you cannot handle him. I feel that I am a total failure. I did not sleep at all last night.

Donna and her husband struggled with Benny for two more years after that incident. A few years later Donna told me: "God alone knows how much we prayed for Benny. Today he is a responsible young man, and we are proud of what he is doing with his life. I am so thankful for that group of parents who supported us during our crisis."

When children choose to let addictions take over their lives, to engage in unethical business practices, to hurt others, or to hurt themselves, parents who care feel great pain and even shame. However, the actions of the children do not necessarily make the parents failures. If a parent's success were to be dependent solely on the choices the children make, God himself would be a great failure. Consider how Adam and Eve acted. They chose to disregard God's parental request in order to follow their own selfish aspiration to be like him. Although Adam and Eve disobeyed, God is not a failure and neither are you! He continues to look after his children and he stands by them no matter what they do. This is the parental model we can emulate.

In this, and the previous five chapters we have examined the path of love, the blueprint to marital happiness. We have highlighted the behaviors and the attitudes that build, maintain, and strengthen the marital relationship: acceptance, commitment, sacrifice, forgiveness, healing, and service. When you follow this path you find the joy that your heart dreams. As you know, growing in self-giving love is not easy. It is a gradual process of emptying oneself to make room for the other. This journey has days that are full of light and warmth, and feel like the ecstatic vision of the apostles on the day of the Transfiguration. This journey, however, also has days that feel like walking with Jesus on the way to Calvary. Many find it difficult to stay on course, and you may at times feel discouraged. As you encounter difficulties remember that you are never alone. God stands by you ready to help you with his graces, but you must open yourself to welcome him and to listen to him. One way to do this is through prayer. The role of prayer in your life will be the subject of the next chapter.

▶ SIMPLE ACTS YOU CAN DO TODAY

1. Today notice three things your spouse does for your benefit and the benefit of your family. Remember to say "Thank you."

2. Take a moment to remind yourself of what your priorities are.

3. Find one opportunity to remind your children of your family's rules, and find behaviors you can praise and affirm.

4. Take a moment to thank God for the gift that your spouse and your children are to you.

▶ LISTEN TO GOD'S STORY

Mary accepts God's call: Luke 1:38
Joseph accepts his servant role: Matthew 1:18–25
The flight into Egypt: Matthew 2:13–15
A trying time for Mary and Joseph: Luke 2:41–52

▶ REFLECT ON YOUR STORY

» List on a piece of paper all the ways your spouse serves you and your family each day.

» Consider the conflicts you experience each day between your roles as parents and your work commitments outside your home. Are you comfortable with how you deal with these conflicts? Do you ever wonder if your priorities are in the right order?

» Are you feeling okay with your parenting style? Do you provide your children the guidance and leadership God expects of you or are you just their maid and chauffeur?

» You have learned many lessons in parenting through your personal experience. What is the most important piece of parenting advice you wish you could pass on to your children as they grow up and become parents? Write this down and share it with your spouse.

» What are your dreams for your children?

» As a servant of God, talk to him and ask him to give you some honest feedback on your performance. Listen to what he says to you.

ENDNOTES

1. *The Rites of the Catholic Church as Revised by the Second Vatican Ecumenical Council*, Study Edition, p. 560. The Catholic Church considers the sacraments of Holy Orders and Matrimony as sacraments at the service of communion. It is through the ministries of those dedicated to these services that Christ serves his church and builds it up. The *Catechism of the Catholic Church* states: "[These sacraments] confer a particular mission in the church and serve to build up the People of God" (#1534). It states also: "Those who receive the sacrament of Holy Orders are consecrated in Christ's name 'to feed the church by the word and grace of God.' On their part, 'Christian spouses are fortified and, as if were, consecrated for the duties and dignity of their state by a special sacrament'" (#1535).

2. http//:www.floridakid.com/inspirations.htm.

3. "We are hardwired to help each other. This has helped us survive as a species for the past several hundred thousand years." Ornish, Dean, M.D., *Love and Survival*, p. 130.

4. According to this author service in marriage means: "Doing things you know your spouse would like you to do." Chapman, Gary, *The Five Love Languages*, pp. 87, 88.

5. John Paul II, *Letter to Families*, #8.

6. Champlin, Joseph, M, *Together for Life*, p.74.

7. "The family is the first and fundamental school of social living: As a community of love, it finds in self-giving the law that guides it and makes it grow." #37. "Thus the fostering of authentic and mature communion between persons within the family is the first and irreplaceable school of social life, an example and stimulus for the broader community of relationships marked by respect, justice, dialogue and love." John Paul II, *Familiaris Consortio*, #43.

8. "Parents are the first and most important educators of their own children." #16. "It is not an exaggeration to reaffirm that the life of nations, of states and of international organizations 'pass' through the family." John Paul II, *Letter to Families*, #15.

9. Doherty, William J. *Take Back Your Marriage*. New York: The Guilford Press, 2001, p. 51.

10. Fagan, Patrick F. and Robert E. Rector. *The Effect of Divorce on America*. The Heritage Foundation, 2003.

11. Duenwald, Mary. (2002, March 26). *2 Portraits of Children of Divorce: Rosy and Dark*, http://listarchives.his.com/smartmarriages/smartmarriages.0203/msg00038.html

12. Marquardt, Elisabeth. *Between Two Worlds: The Inner Lives of Children of Divorce*. New York: Three River Press, 2006.
    Elisabeth Marquardt states in a summary of her book published on the website (http://betweentwoworlds.org/comments/) that children of divorce who stay in touch with both parents must become travelers between two very different worlds. When parents are married it is their primary responsibility to reconcile the two worlds which each brings to the marriage and to deal with the conflicts that arise from these differences. By contrast, writes Marquardt, when parents divorce they each retreat to live in their own worlds, which over time become increasingly different and even with divorce conflicts do not disappear. At this point, unfortunately, the job of making sense of the conflicts that exist in the two worlds between which the child is caught falls entirely on the child alone.

13. The Catholic Church does not favor divorce. Even when a marriage is in serious trouble, the church's preference is always that the marriage be saved. But, there are situations where the church acknowledges and tolerates the reality of separation and civil divorce. For example, the *Catechism of the Catholic Church* (#2383) says: "The separation of spouses while maintaining the marriage bond can be legitimate in certain cases provided for by canon law." These cases are listed in several places in the Code of Canon law, including Canon 1153: "If either of the spouses causes serious danger of spirit or body to the other spouse or to the children...that spouse gives the other a legitimate cause for separating...." The *Catechism* goes on to say that "if civil divorce remains the only possible way of ensuring certain legal rights, the care of the children, or the protection of inheritance, it can be tolerated and does not constitute a moral offense" (#2383).

14. "The study found no evidence that unhappily married adults who divorce were typically any happier than unhappily married people who stayed married." The authors pose the question, why did some marriages survive where others did not? There seem to be three reasons why unhappy marriages survived: 1. Some spouses stubbornly outlasted their problems. Time changed the situations and the relationship became happier. 2. Some spouses identified the problems and worked at solving them. 3. Some spouses accepted the limitations of their marriage and found alternative ways to build a good and happy life together.
    Also: Waite, Linda J., Don Browning, William J. Doherty, Maggie Gallagher, Ye Lou, and Scott M. Stanley. "Does Marriage Make People Happy?" Press Release, http://www.americanvalues.org/html/r-unhappy_ii.html.

CHAPTER 11

Where Do I Find the Courage?

"The Eucharist is the very source of Christian marriage. The Eucharistic Sacrifice represents Christ's covenant of love with the church."

■ *FAMILIARIS CONSORTIO, #57*

"Damned if you do, and damned if you don't."

Jim* said to me:

In the early years of my marriage, there were many times when I wondered where our relationship was going. I loved my wife immensely, and I knew we were meant to be together for all of our life. But, from time to time our relationship seemed hopeless. She would be overcome by very dark moods, filled with anger

*name has been changed

144

and distant silence that went on for days. I didn't know if she was upset with me, or unhappy to be married. I took her negativity personally and felt insulted. When this happened, it created a chasm between us, which I found impossible to cross.

On those occasions, the harder I tried to reach out to her the more she would hide behind a wall of silence. If I pulled away, she would claim I didn't care, and her mood would become even darker. This was a "damned if you do, damned if you don't" type of situation. I felt helpless because I was caught up in her struggle. The questions would often arise in my mind: "What am I doing here?" "Why put up with this?" And, in the moments of deep anger and frustration, thoughts of separation and divorce crossed my mind. However, I never gave them serious consideration. I felt that my commitment to her was irrevocable. I knew that we belonged together, and we had to make this relationship work, although at times, it was hard to see how this was possible.

Marge* and I later learned that her moods and behaviors were triggered by the Pre-Menstrual Syndrome (PMS). I knew, therefore, that these storms were temporary. Even so, I found it hard to cope. These episodes took a toll on our relationship. My reaction to her moods would be frustration and anger, which created distance between us. Then, when the storms passed over, it would take a while to get close to each other again. And, these hurts were taking longer and longer to heal.

One day, as I wrestled one more time with the question: "What am I doing here?" I recognized that my wife was in pain, a pain I could not soothe. I also realized my own helplessness in changing my wife's feelings and behaviors. At that moment I had two choices. I could give up, or I could turn to a higher power, God, for help. Guided by my faith, I turned to God in prayer.

From then on, when these episodes appeared, I did my best not to aggravate the situation. Most of all, I prayed to God not for myself but for Marge. I prayed to God to give her peace. I prayed to God to give me patience. I prayed to God to calm her anger and depression, to ease her burden, and to guide her. I prayed to God to keep my love for her alive. That was my way of disengaging from the double-bind in which the two of us were trapped. It was my only way to express my love for her and stay positive. Those prayers, I believe, helped me cope. Praying also gave me the courage to discuss this situation with Marge. In a moment of calm, I told her we needed to talk to someone who could help us avoid these hurtful incidents. Together we agreed to seek medical help and marriage counseling.

Over the years, our relationship has grown. The storms have become fewer. Medical intervention has helped and counseling has taught us new skills for coping. I love my wife very much and all of those pains are but distant memories. I am thankful to God for my faith. It has been a source of great strength and guidance in our relationship.

All couples go through similar crises and challenges from time to time. Perhaps you have been through a situation like this. We learned in previous chapters that what keeps spouses together, even during hard times, is the goodness they see in each other. In this chapter we will explore another powerful force that keeps couples together and helps them grow in their relationship. This force can keep spouses engaged in their marriage even when they have lost sight of each other's goodness and the goodness of their relationship. This force is the power of prayer inspired by the Christian faith. This is what Jim and his wife learned during their ordeal.

In your moments of crisis, you, like Jim, can reach beyond yourself to find guidance and strength in God. Prayer allows you to look at your spouse and at your relationship from God's perspective. Through prayer you can find the courage to stay turned toward your spouse and to continue to work on your marriage, even if it is hard.

▶ PRAYER IS YOUR NOURISHMENT

Prayer is to your marriage what food is to your body. Prayer is the spiritual food that your relationship needs because the interpersonal communion you are trying to create in your marriage is a spiritual reality. Prayer, whether said alone or together, has the power to strengthen your bond. Joachim Wach, a noted author of the history of religions, wrote that there is no stronger bond between two people than being bound together in God.[1] A 1999 study conducted by the Ministry to Interchurch Marriages has found that joint religious activity by husband and wife is a significant predictor of marital stability.[2]

You may think of prayer as something boring because you may associate praying with the recitation of formal prayers: the Rosary, Novenas, and reading the Psalms. Praying does not have to be boring. The simplest way to pray is to be aware of your own feelings and emotions and let these be an invitation to lift your heart and mind to God.

I know a mother who is very much aware of her feelings and uses them to remind herself of God's presence in her life. On days when her husband travels or on evenings when her teenage children are out late, her feelings of anxiety and concern for the well-being of her family prompt her to turn to God for assistance and protection. She lights a candle that she keeps in a prominent spot in the kitchen. The flickering light is a reminder to her that God is watching over her family and she can stop worrying. This is prayer.

Rabbi Abraham J. Heschel, a respected Jewish philosopher and mystic, writes: "Feelings become prayer in the moment in which we forget ourselves and become aware of God"[3] Your feelings of awe, fear, joy, sadness, anger, frustration, and even depression are doorways to God. God awaits you in the depth of your heart, at the threshold of your emotions.[4] In the stressful moments of your life you can choose to ignore God's presence. If you do, you will be all alone with your pain and frustrations. On the other hand, if you turn to God and open your heart to him his presence will comfort you and give you strength.

A young wife and mother of three told me recently that during her long days of caring for her toddlers at home and doing family chores she finds strength and courage from her conversations with God. She told me, "When something bothers me, I speak to God. When I am pleased by the progress I see in my young children, I speak to God and thank him. He is my daily companion. I talk to him, I ask him for advice. At times I even express my frustrations and anger toward him. He keeps me sane, and his presence in my life keeps me going."

The private prayer life of Catholic families is rich and varied. Some spouses pray alone, others pray together. Some use spontaneous words to pray; others prefer to use more formal and traditional prayers such as the Our Father or the Hail Mary. In their prayers many are aware of the Catholic Church's belief in the Communion of Saints. This communion is the kinship that exists among all those who believe in Christ, whether they are alive here on Earth, or in Heaven. Because of this, couples pray to Mary, to the saints, and even to family members and friends who have died. They pray asking them to intercede to God on their behalf.

▶ VIATICUM

During a business trip to Spain, I had the opportunity of spending one afternoon at the famous Prado art museum in Madrid. As I wandered from room to room admiring masterpieces by Velasquez, Goya, Murillo, Rubens, Van Dyck, and many others I came upon a small canvas that caught my attention. It was a painting created in 1636 called "El Viatico en una iglesia" by Pieter Neefs. The canvas depicts the inside of a large gothic style church. Processing down the nave of the church there is a small cluster of persons walking toward the exit. The main figure in this group is a priest who is carrying the Blessed Sacrament. Four altar boys dressed in clerical garb and carrying candles surround him. They are taking communion, the Body of Christ, to the sick of the parish. As I stared at this scene I was transported back to my childhood when, during the summer, after serving morning Mass in my parish church, I used to escort my pastor to take the "Viaticum" to the sick parishioners. "Viaticum" is a Latin word, which refers to the provisions that are used in a journey. "Viaticum" is the food travelers take with them to give them strength and to sustain them on their journey.

▶ THE EUCHARIST

The Eucharist, as a prayer, is every married couple's Viaticum for the journey they are making together. The Mass is the perfect nourishment for the marital journey because the Eucharist is the celebration of divine love, the matrix of human love. Pope Benedict XVI, when he was still Cardinal Ratzinger, wrote: "In the Eucharist a communion takes place that corresponds to the union of man and woman in marriage. Just as they become 'one flesh', so in Communion we all become 'one spirit', one person in Christ."[5] In the rites of the Mass we walk with Christ the path of love that leads to union with God and one another. Through these rituals the loving relationship of Christ for his bride, the church is enacted and celebrated: Christ, the high priest, welcomes us, reminds us of God's commitment to being present to us, sacrifices himself for us, forgives our sins, heals our pains, and sends us out into the world to serve God and one another.

Every time spouses participate in the celebration of the Eucharist together they have an opportunity to worship God and to strengthen their bond. Mass is for husband and wife a clear invitation to love each other as Christ loves the church and thus be transformed. Ratzinger explains: "It has always been clear that the goal of the Eucharist is our own transformation, so that we become 'one body and spirit' with Christ."[6]

In the remainder of this chapter we will explore how the rites of the Mass are a celebration of Christ's love and are a summons to spouses to communion with Christ and one another. They are an invitation to husband and wife to renew the commitment to each other made on their wedding day; the commitment to welcome each other, to always be present, to make sacrifices for the sake of their relationship, to forgive, to help each other heal, and to serve one another.

▶ THE GREETING AND WELCOMING RITE

The priest opens the Mass with a welcoming prayer and a gesture through which he invites us to open our hearts to welcome God and one another. Representing Christ, the priest extends his arms toward the congregation as if to embrace everyone while he says: "The Lord be with you." And we respond: "And also with you." I once belonged to a parish where, upon the invitation of the priest, those gathered turned towards the people standing nearby to greet them and to introduce themselves to them. This gesture is a sign of welcome, and it is the recognition that we are not there as individuals gathered to pray privately, but as a community to worship the Father together with his Son, Jesus, and the Holy Spirit.

When you attend Mass, especially if you are with your spouse, let this be the moment in which you make a special effort to remember your wedding promise to welcome and accept your spouse into your life. At your wedding you said: "I take you to be my spouse." Today, you stand by your spouse, much more aware than on your wedding day of what it means to welcome and accept this unique person. You know your spouse's strengths and weaknesses; you know what you like about this individual and what you do not like. As you join the congregation in responding to the welcome of the priest, open your heart to your spouse and renew your commitment to welcome him or her into your life. Thank God for the happiness your spouse brings to you, and ask for God's help to accept your mate as he or she is even with the imperfections that cause you discomfort from time to time.

▶ THE PENITENTIAL RITE

After acknowledging Christ's welcome to this communal celebration, we are invited to recognize our sinfulness and our need for forgiveness. As a community we ask God for his mercy. We say together: *"Kyrie Eleison—Lord have mercy."* As a sinful people we recite the prayer of repentance, often referred to as the Confiteor. Through it we admit our shortcomings, our failings toward God, toward our brothers and sisters, including our spouse, and we promise to correct our failings.

The next time you are at Mass with your spouse, try to consciously be aware of the words you are saying. You will hear yourself saying something like this: I confess to almighty God and to you, my brothers and sisters (husband/wife) that I have sinned...I made mistakes. They are my fault. I am sorry. Please forgive me. Pray for me and help me avoid these in the future.

Too often you may not think about what you are saying as you recite these prayers. When you pay attention and truly mean what you say, you find yourself moved by the grace of God. Your heart is softened and your intolerance and judgmental attitude toward your spouse melt away. You let go of the grudges, the resentments, and the anger you may feel. You ask for forgiveness and you forgive. At that moment, the barriers that stand between you and God, and between you and your spouse are removed. Your communion is restored. You are ready as a couple and as members of God's family to celebrate and worship God as one. Then, you sit down and prepare to listen to God speak to you and guide you with his Word, which is about to be proclaimed.

▶ THE LITURGY OF THE WORD

Through the proclamation of sacred text from the Old and the New Testament God tells us of his enduring love and commitment to humanity. The Old Testament passages speak to us of God's care for his chosen people, Israel. The New Testament readings tell us of how Christ loves his church. He says to us: I am with you and I have loved you even to the point of dying for you. Love one another as I have loved you because it is in loving that you will find God's peace and joy.

As you listen to God speak to us, his church, let his word touch your heart. Hear about God's unwavering faithfulness and about the truth contained in his message. Let God's word guide you in keeping your commitment to always be present and truthful to your spouse.

▶ EXPRESSING APPRECIATION

The second part of the Mass is known as the liturgy of the Eucharist. The rite begins the offertory and with a song of thanksgiving through which we sing our praises to God and express our appreciation to the Father for the gift of his Son. The celebrant proclaims in these or similar words: "Father, all powerful and ever-living God, we do well always and everywhere to give you thanks and praise....In wonder and gratitude, we join our voices with the choirs of heaven to proclaim the power of your love and to sing of our salvation in Christ: Holy, Holy, Holy Lord, God of power and might....Hosanna in the highest."[7]

During this part of the Mass when you join the congregation in giving praise and thanks to God, think about how you express your gratitude to your spouse. One of the main problems in marriages comes from the fact that spouses take each other for granted. We know how much our spouse gives to the relationship, but often we do not acknowledge our beloved's giving, and by taking it for granted, our mutual connection loses energy. We gradually drift apart. Resolve to say "thank you" to your spouse for everything he or she does for you. Appreciation is not expressed only in words. It can be said with a smile, a touch, a special glance, a note, a kiss, and in many other ways.

▶ THE CONSECRATION— CELEBRATING CHRIST'S SACRIFICE

The priest continues the recitation of the Eucharistic prayer. He recounts God's many acts of love toward humanity, culminating with the gift of his

Son and his death on the cross. The consecration follows during which the words said by Christ at the Last Supper are repeated over the bread and wine, that become the body and blood of Christ.

Christ, who is present, says to us: "Take this, all of you, and eat it: this is my body which is given up for you...." Then, as the priest raises the cup, Christ says: "Take this, all of you, and drink from it: this is the cup of my blood,...It will be shed for you...." The words of Christ at the consecration: "Take this...which is given up for you" contain the core elements of true love, self-giving, and accepting. Christ is giving himself fully for us, so that we can experience the intimacy and communion with God and one another as it was before Adam's sin. We receive his generous gift and accept it exclaiming with joy as a community: "Amen, Amen, Amen."

The Eucharist ritual reminds us that, to follow Christ's example, we must be willing to give and to make sacrifices for the good of the relationship. Ask yourself: Am I giving my spouse the attention I promised? Am I being honest with my spouse as I said I would? Am I sharing with my spouse my thoughts, my wishes, my plans? Am I willing to listen without interrupting so that I can understand what my spouse wants and thinks? Am I willing to make compromises when my spouse and I have a conflict? Am I willing to take the first step in making peace when we have a disagreement? This list is endless. Remember that the giving and the receiving that goes on each day in a marriage are the essence of your love. Improving the quality of this mutual self-giving is the secret to your marital happiness. Ultimately, to follow Christ, you need to rid yourself of your selfishness.

▶ THE COMMUNION RITE

After having joined Christ in offering his sacrifice to the Father we proclaim our unity as members of God's family in the recitation of the "Our Father." In this prayer we recognize that we are all brothers and sisters in Christ; we are children of God who are hungry and in need of his nourishment. We pray: "Our Father...Thy kingdom come, Thy will be done...Give us this day our daily bread..." We ask God to give us the food that can sustain us and heal us.

The sign of peace is a moving ritual. It is a visible sign of the communion that exists among the members of God's family. It was once called "The Kiss of Peace." Have you ever noticed how the whole congregation becomes energized when people reach out to one another to shake hands? They smile and say: "Peace be with you." Friends embrace. Couples kiss. This ritual gives us a glimpse of the spiritual energy generated when people connect with each other to acknowledge, and to express their interpersonal communion among themselves and with God.

For you and your spouse, if you are at Mass together, this is a great moment of unity. It is a physical and public expression of your spiritual unity and love for each other. This sign of peace is one more chance to tear down the obstacles that may stand between the two of you and to truly mean what you say when you tell each other: "Peace be with you."

This unity as a couple and as a community becomes even more real when you and your spouse receive the Body of Christ at the Communion Rite. You are truly affirmed as one in Christ. I have seen many spouses, especially those who have attended a Marriage Encounter weekend, approach the Eucharistic Minister side by side to receive communion together. This act is a visible and public manifestation of their union in Christ, and their communion with each other.

When you and your spouse participate in the Mass and let the grace that comes from these rituals open your hearts to God and to each other, you leave the celebration of the Eucharist fed and nourished spiritually. You feel energized because the barriers that existed and were sapping the relationship have been torn down; your hearts have been opened to God and to each other; your union has been strengthened. You cannot be against each other if you are united in God. Thus, you are ready to continue your journey on the path of love with a stronger resolve.

▶ THE DISMISSAL

The grace received during the celebration of the Mass does not stay within the confines of the church building. Couples carry these blessings with them when they leave to go home. In fact, the rite of the Mass does not end with the ritual of Holy Communion. It ends with a special dismissal. The priest, speaking for Christ, closes the Mass with the exhortation: "Go in peace to love and serve the Lord."[8] We are sent out as a community to serve God in what we do, and to love others as Christ loves us, and we respond: "Thanks be to God."

When at home, a touch, a look, a gesture, a kind word, a silent pause, a smile, are all behaviors that resonate God's love celebrated at Mass. They convey messages to your spouse that say: "It's okay. I don't mind." "You are important to me." "I trust you." "You are part of my life." "You can count on me!" "Please forgive me." "I care about you." "How can I help you?" Each of these messages is an expression of love that flows from your communion with God to create a communion between persons in marriage. Your acts of love keep the communion that exists between you and your spouse growing and spreads to your family and to your neighborhood. Your interactions have a sacramental power. Each of your actions touches the other person in a way that gives your spouse a taste of the goodness of God's love.

Through your faith you acknowledge the presence of the Spirit of God in your life and invite him to aid you in your daily effort to love your spouse. He gives you the wisdom to understand and to accept your spouse, the fortitude to live up to your promises, the generosity to give unselfishly, the willingness to forgive, the compassion to heal and console, and the dedication to always serve without expecting to be served. Your life is filled with divine energy.

Prayer, whether private or public is the force that will keep you together. Prayer is the nourishment that gives you strength when you feel weak. It is the food that gives you courage to persevere when you feel like running away. Prayer is not something difficult; it is talking to God. Prayer is asking God for his advice and help. Prayer is giving God thanks and praise for the joys you experience together. Remember that God is the matrix of human love. He made you to love the way he loves, and when you do you "become what you are," fulfilling God's design, you give glory to God, and you feel great joy.

Christ tells us of the joy we experience when you love the way he loves: "This is my commandment, that you love one another as I have loved you... I have said these things to you so that my joy may be in you, and that your joy may be complete" (Jn 15:11–12).

▶ SIMPLE ACTS YOU CAN DO TODAY

» Today, be aware of your feelings, positive or negative, pleasant or painful, and let them prompt you to turn your mind to God.

» Today, when your spouse does something that irritates you, ask God to help you speak to your spouse in a way that does not escalate the tension.

» Resolve that you will attend Mass with your spouse next Sunday. Then, pay attention to how the participation in this sacrament helps you love your spouse.

» Pray to God for help in becoming the gift to your spouse that he made you to be.

▶ LISTEN TO GOD'S STORY

How to pray: Matthew 6:5–15
The institution of the Eucharist: Matthew 26:26–30

▶ REFLECT ON YOUR STORY

» What are the key ideas that stand out in your mind after reading this chapter? What is it that you want to remember about this chapter?

» What is the most comfortable way for you to pray?

» Do you pray as a couple? If so, when and how?

» What practices do you have in your home that prompt you to pray or help you pray? For example, do you pray before meals? Do you pray before bedtime or in the morning?

» Do you regularly attend Mass together with your spouse? If you do not, consider the changes you need to make in your priorities and schedule so that your marriage can benefit by your participation in the Eucharist.

» What have you learned about the Mass from this chapter that can help you participate in it more fully?

▶ ENDNOTES

1. Wach, Joachim. *The Comparative Study of Religions*. New York: Columbia University Press, 1958, p. 125.

2. cmfce@smartmarriages.com, online newsletter.

3. Heschel, Abraham J. *Man's Quest for God*. New York: Charles Scribner's Sons, 1954, p. 15.

4. "God who probes the heart awaits for him there." Abbott, *Documents of Vatican II: The Church Today*. New York: Guild Press, 1966, #14.

5. Ratzinger, Cardinal Joseph. *The Spirit of the Liturgy*. San Francisco: Ignatius Press, 2000, p. 142.

6. Ratzinger, Cardinal Joseph, *The Spirit of the Liturgy*, p. 86.

7. *The Roman Missal. Eucharistic Prayer for Masses of Reconciliation I,* 1975.

8. The Mass "concludes with the sending forth (*Missio*) of the faithful, so that they may fulfill God's will in their lives." *Catechism of the Catholic Church,* #1332.

They Lived Happily Ever After

"In the joys of their love and family life he gives them here on earth a foretaste of the wedding feast of the Lamb."

■ *CATECHISM OF THE CATHOLIC CHURCH*[1]

All couples walk out of the wedding chapel aspiring to live happily ever after, as childhood fairy tales proclaim. Married life is a life lived in the pursuit of happiness, but finding it requires effort.

Steve* and Lisa* are a couple that could be anyone's grandparents or neighbors. From what you see of them they fit together like a hand in a glove. As you watch them, you can see that over the years, they have figured

*name has been changed

each other out, and have arrived at an arrangement between them that is comfortable for both. They are happy together. She knows all of his idiosyncrasies and plays along with them. He knows her weaknesses and protects her. She knows how much sugar and cream he likes in his coffee and prepares it for him. He knows her habits and accommodates her. He sets the clock in the bedroom ten minutes fast so that when they go out they arrive at functions on time. She knows it and appreciates it because it helps her. They go for walks together; they travel to see their grandchildren in different parts of the country. They enjoy each other's company and watch their favorite shows together. They have individual friends and friends in common. They know each other's hot buttons and could push these at any moment, but they choose not to.

This couple was not always so comfortable with each other. There were times when their differences created major conflicts. In the first years of their marriage they battled vehemently over small things. They tried to change each other. At times, they even hurt each other. However, with time, they have learned that it is better to be patient, to accept, to accommodate, and to compromise, than to fight. They know that ultimately no one else cares about you more than your spouse. Therefore, arguments have gradually subsided. However, from time to time, you can hear one of them roar at the other. They are like lions that need to remind themselves that they are still lions. Afterwards, they go back to being the best of friends, and faithful companions. They are a "we" and would not know what to do without each other.

▶ THE JOURNEY TO LOVE

Michele Weiner-Davis, author of many books on marriage, describes five stages in the evolution of marital relationships. Stage one: Passion Prevails. Stage two: What was I thinking? Stage three: Everything would be great if you changed. Stage four: That's just the way he/she is. Stage five: Together at last.[2]

Reaching stage five is a long journey for all couples. A critical skill that spouses need in order to progress on this journey is managing the changes they must make to accommodate each other's needs and be comfortable in each other's company. Unfortunately, this is the reason many of us do not make progress on the journey to love. We resist making changes. We prefer to keep doing what we do. We keep our own habits and preferences, and persist in our own ideas, even if these cause conflicts in the relationship. The comfort of keeping our own views and our habits often outweighs the discomfort that they bring to the relationship.

Instead of changing our own behaviors we expect our spouse to change. Instead of obliging our partner we want our mate to accept our idiosyncrasies, our preferences, and our wishes. This is a problem because our spouse hates to change just as much as we do. And so, we play games with each other that keep us from growing in love. Sometimes our life resembles a tug-of-war; other times it's a food fight. Each person blames the other for the pain we feel.

▶ IT BEGINS WITH ME

To make progress on the journey to love you must make changes. Don't wait for your spouse to change. Change must begin with you.

If you wonder where to start, I recommend that you begin where you know there is pain in the relationship. Change must start with you regardless of whether you are the person who feels the pain or not. Always take the first step by replacing your behaviors and attitudes with the loving behaviors you learned from Christ in the pages of this book. For example:

> » Where there is sarcasm and impatience introduce kindness and tolerance.

> » Where there is misunderstanding seek to understand.

> » Where you find that you are ignoring your spouse show attentiveness.

> » Where you find that you are not being forthright be truthful.

» Where you act with a self-centered attitude learn to be magnanimous and be willing to sacrifice what you want.

» Where you find that you have hurt your spouse ask forgiveness.

» Where you have been hurt offer your forgiveness.

» Where there is stress or physical pain offer support and compassion.

» Where your spouse needs help don't hesitate to offer a hand.

There may be times, however, when the changes you make stir up conflicts instead of bringing peace. Out of love you may need to challenge your spouse and confront certain behaviors. This is often the most difficult for some couples. Unfortunately many spouses who find themselves in this situation are afraid to introduce any change. Some suffer in silence because they fear that confrontation will have a worse outcome. The fact is that this martyrdom syndrome is a major obstacle on your journey to love. If you feel that you are one of these spouses, seek professional help to guide you on how to get unstuck from this love-sapping situation.

▶ YOUR FAITH WILL HELP YOU

The energy you need to make changes and to grow in love comes from your Christian faith. Your openness to God in faith brings the many graces you need. Faith helps you to turn to the Holy Spirit to ask for courage to overcome your selfish tendencies, guidance to take the first step in making changes, humility to seek and understand your spouse, and wisdom to say and do what is right.

As you travel this journey remember that you and your spouse are imperfect. No matter how hard you try you will never be able to fully satisfy each other's need for love. Your desire for intimacy and joy will never be completely fulfilled in this lifetime. Your heart hungers for a happiness and communion that can only be satisfied in God's presence, in the next life. St. Augustine expressed this very eloquently when he wrote: "O God, you have made us for yourself, and our heart is restless until it rests in you."[3]

▶ THE FINAL DESTINATION

The Christian faith teaches that each person's voyage extends beyond the journey on earth and beyond the boundaries of time.[4] You are destined to be in communion with God[5] in whom alone you find happiness.[6] Dr. Dean Ornish, the renowned cardiologist, says it well when he writes: "The most fundamental longing of the human heart is for union with the Divine."[7]

When you look at marriage guided by the Christian faith you see that what man and woman seek to experience in marriage is a taste, although imperfect, of the communion that they desire with God. James Penrice writes: "Marriage is a temporary institution helping us on our earthly journey to get a glimpse of God whom we will see fully in heaven."[8]

The feelings of joy and pleasure that you cherish in your spouse's embrace are a preview of the immense happiness you will experience when you meet God face to face and are held in his loving arms. The *Catechism of the Catholic Church* reminds us: "In the joys of their love and family life he gives them here on earth a foretaste of the wedding feast of the Lamb." [9] Marriage is a journey to communion with each other that leads to God.[10]

I close this book with the blessing that the minister prays over the couple after they have proclaimed their vows at a Catholic wedding:

> *May God, the almighty Father, give you his joy*
> *and bless you in your children.*
> *May the only Son of God have mercy on you*
> *and help you in good times and in bad.*
> *May the Holy Spirit of God*
> *always fill your hearts with his love.*
> *And may almighty God bless you all,*
> *the Father, and the Son, and the Holy Spirit.*
> *Amen.*[11]

▶ ENDNOTES

1. *Catechism of the Catholic Church*, #1642.

2. Weiner-Davis, Michele. "Navigating the Marriage Map," *Parade* Magazine. March 17, 2002.

3. St. Augustine: *Confessions*, Book I. Paragraph 1.

4. "In God's plan, however, the vocation of the human person extends beyond the boundaries of time." John Paul II, *Letter to Families*, #9.

5. "All men are called to one and the same goal, namely, God Himself." Abbott, *Documents of Vatican II: The Church Today*, #24.

6. "Man is made to live in communion with God in whom he finds happiness." *Catechism of the Catholic Church*, #45.
    Also: "And thus it (the human intellect) will have its perfection through union with God...in which alone man's happiness consists." Aquinas, Thomas. *Summa Theologiae*. First Part of Second Part, Treatise on the Last End (Happiness), Question 3, Article 8.

7. Ornish, Dean, MD, *Love and Survival*, p. 141.

8. Penrice, James. *You Know More Than You Think*. New York,: Alba House, 2003, p. 51.

9. *Catechism of the Catholic Church*, #1642.

10. "Authentic married love is caught up into divine love. Thus this love can lead the spouses to God." Abbott, *Documents Of Vatican II, The Church Today*, #48.

11. Champlin, Joseph M., *Together for Life*, p. 84.